Practical Course In
MODERN SHOE REPAIRING

By Ralph E. Sarlette
MASTER CRAFTSMAN

*A Benj. Franklin Illustrated Home-Study
Course Complete in One Volume*

NELSON-HALL CO., *Publishers*
CHICAGO, U. S. A.

F O R E W O R D

Shoe repairing is an old and honored trade. It is a profitable trade, and can be learned readily. Pa - tience, alertness, neatness, and common sense are the main qualifications.

The repair of the shoe consists of the following steps, all of which are described and illustrated fully in this manual:

1. Preparation of materials to be used.

2. Preparation of the shoe.

3. Attaching the sole.

   A. Sewing

   B. Nailing

   C. Stapling

   D. Cementing

4. Attaching the Heel.

5. Finishing the sole edge.

6. Finishing the heel edge.

7. Repairing the loose seams and patching holes in the uppers.

LESSONS

LESSON I

STANDARD MATERIALS USED IN SHOE CONSTRUCTION

Practically all shoes, including men's, women's and children's, are made of three materials - - leather, cloth and rubber.

Each shoe is divided into two distinct parts, namely; the upper and the bottom.

Leather is made (tanned) from the hides (skins) of practically every kind of animal. The leathers used for the uppers and bottoms of shoes may come from the same type of animals. The difference in thickness, flexibility and color is brought about by the different formulas used in the tanning of the hides.

In this course we will not attempt to go into detail about leathers but we would advise the student to obtain encyclopedias and various other volumes on leather, and study them thoroughly. One cannot become a master craftsman without full knowledge of the entire craft.

1. UPPER MATERIALS

    A - The majority of men's shoes are made of calfskin. Kangaroo and kid leather are also used but mostly in shoes for older men and for men with tender feet.

    B - Ladies' shoes are made from a variety of materials but the most predominant are calfskin, kid and suede leathers. Novelty shoes for women are made usually of alligator leather, patent leather and satin, with a few made of various types of cloth.

    C - Children's shoes are practically all made of calfskin.

2. BOTTOM MATERIALS

GENERAL: - The materials used for the bottom
(Insoles, Outsoles and Heels) of shoes are divided
into three groups - leather, rubber and plastic.

A - Time and science have proved that the best
material for foot protection is leather. Gran-
ted that other materials may wear longer
than leather but a material that is not porous
does not allow the feet to "breathe" so to
speak.   Feet must have the ventilation which
leather gives.

To attain and retain healthy feet, shoes should
be worn that are constructed to give support
to the feet, and of materials that are porous
and do not stretch with wear. Nothing is more
true than the old saying.   " There is no substitute for leather for foot covering. " It is
suggested that for the good of your customer's
feet you try to "sell" them on leather-soles
whenever possible. Practically all sole lea -
ther is made from cattle hides but a small
percentage is made from horse and buffalo
hides.

B - In recent year various forms of rubber and
rubber composition soles have become popu -
lar.   This has been brought about because
rubber soles, as a rule, will outwear leather
and because of a greater shortage of leather
than rubber during the War. Although rubber
soles will outwear leather you will find that
the average person cannot wear rubber soles
for any length of time. To some people rubber soles cause a "burning" feeling to their
feet; to others, rubber soles cause their feet
to perspire more; to still others rubber soles
cause cold feet in chilly weather.

C - Plastic materials for shoe bottoming are relatively new to the industry and to date are merely a substitute for leather and rubber . At the present time plastics are only mildly successful. It is recommended that the student wait until they have been proven successful before adopting them to use for resoling.

D - Recommendations for materials used for reheeling are just the opposite of those for resoling. Rubber heels are, by far, more popular than leather, and rightfully so.

The student will be wise in recommending rubber heels to his customers, first, because they are more healthful; and second, because they will wear longer. The heel of the shoe gets the entire weight of the wearer's body in each step and as a result the rubber heel serves as a cushion or shock absorber to the spine. Wearers of solid leather heels jar their spine with each step as there is no "give" in the leather heel. By the same token the heel gets two to three times the wear that the sole does.

E - Regardless of what materials you use remember always that there is no substitute for quality. There are on the market both good and poor leather and rubber heels and soles.

There are only two ways to get business; one is selling the customer quality materials and service; the other is selling through "price". Building a business on quality is slow at the beginning however it is a more lasting business for it is built on a solid foundation. You establish a business on "resale", for your satisfied customers come back and bring their friends. If you operate a business catering to "price", you will get a customer only once.

A shoe repairman's main product is his services. When he does his work for a cheap price
he is only admitting that he is not as good as
the other fellow. It has been found that the
majority of "price" shoe shops do not stay in
the same locations any length of time.

LESSON   II

HOW   TO   RECOGNIZE   GOOD   SOLE   LEATHER

As previously stated the principal leathers used
for the bottoms of shoes are tanned from the skins of
cattle.

Regardless of the different methods and formulas
used by different tanners, each hide is cut into four
grades of leather, as shown in Figure I.

(FIG. I)

HALF of HIDE or "SIDE"

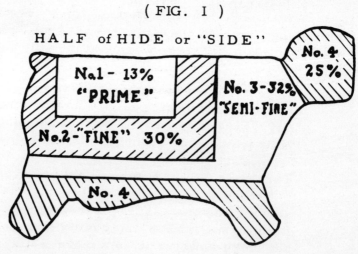

"Prime" Close Fiber   "Semi-Fine"
Best Wear - 13% of Hide   Fair Wear - 32% of Hide

"Fine" - Good Wear   No. 4 - Poor Quality
30% of the hide   25% of the hide

1. - TERMS.   The side of the leather that was next
to the body of the animal is known in the trade as the
FLESH SIDE.   The hair side of the hide is known as
the GRAIN SIDE. The grain side of leather is usually
used as the outside and is processed smooth and finished off.

2. - QUALITY. There are two ways to determine the
quality of a piece of leather if no identification is shown.

    A. - Look at the flesh side of the leather -it will
    be noted that on prime leather veins are very evi-
    dent while in the poorer grades few or no veins
    will be in evidence. Note Figure 2.

(Fig. 2)

QUALITY OF LEATHER

Note presence or absence
of veins on flesh side.

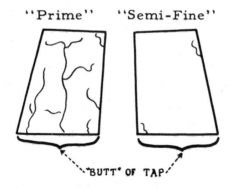

"Prime"   "Semi-Fine"

"BUTT" OF TAP

    B. - The second method in determining the qua-
    lity of leather is to cut a thin slice off the edge. Look
    at the cut edge, if the fibers are close and firm
    you have a good piece of leather. The lesser and
    looser the fibres the poorer the quality of the lea-
    ther with a firm fibre is harder to cut.

3. - TANNAGES. The two most popular tannages for
sole leather are known as Oak and Chrome tannages.

A - Oak tanned soles are more popular because
they can be finished off smoother and with a better
polish. Oak soles are also more adaptable to the
cementing process.   Oak leather is usually a
russet color.

B - Chrome tanned leathers are more water and
wear resistant than Oak leathers. Because
of its wearing qualities Chrome leather is usually
used on work shoes and on children's shoes.
Chrome leather usually has a greenish hue in
color.

(See figure 3 on page 7)

The Bend,   Crop and Back are cut from a Side.
Strips are cut from Bends, Taps and Full Soles are
cut from Strips.

Taps are cut into two general shapes - Angle and
Round. See Figure 4.

As a rule shoe repairmen stock mostly Taps,
Full Soles and Strips. Strips are stocked in order
to cut full soles or taps for shoes too large for standard cuts.

(FIGURES 3 AND 4 ON PAGE 7)

(Fig. 3)

"CUTS" of LEATHER

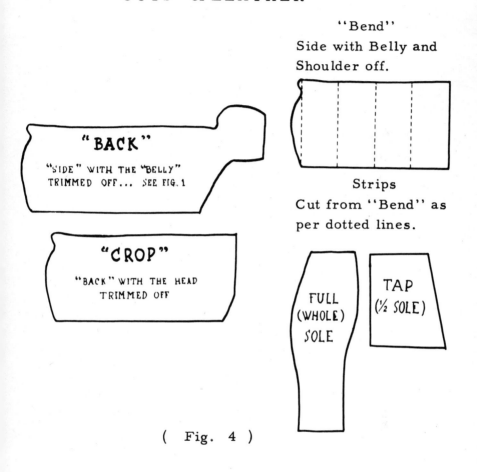

"Bend"
Side with Belly and
Shoulder off.

"BACK"

"SIDE" WITH THE "BELLY"
TRIMMED OFF... SEE FIG. 1

Strips
Cut from "Bend" as
per dotted lines.

"CROP"

"BACK" WITH THE HEAD
TRIMMED OFF

FULL
(WHOLE)
SOLE

TAP
(½ SOLE)

(Fig. 4)

Two Styles of Taps

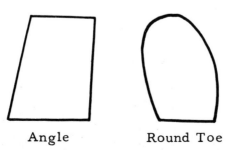

Angle   Round Toe

(Fig. 4)

The length and width of leather are always measured in feet but the thickness is measured in IRONS.
An Iron equals 1/48 of an inch. For example :
12 Iron leather is 12/48 or 1/4 of an inch thick.

All sole leather, except full soles and taps, is
sold by the pound. Full soles and taps are sold by
the dozen.

5. - PURCHASE MATERIALS. All shoe repair materials, tools, machinery, etc., can be obtained
from wholesalers, known in the shoe repair trade as
JOBBERS and/or FINDERS. It is also possible to
purchase or lease tools and machinery direct from
the manufacturer.

There are shoe repair jobbers located in practically all larger cities and practically all have sales-
men on the road so that nearly every hamlet, village,
town and city in the U.S. is contacted and serviced.

Shoe machinery manufacturers have either
branch offices or representatives in all the large
cities of the U.S., Canada and Mexico.

LESSON   III

STANDARD SHOE CONSTRUCTION METHODS

Before the student can repair shoes success-
fully it is important that he know the construction
of the different types of shoes. It is recommended
that the student study shoe construction thoroughly
as he cannot repair any shoe without the full knowledge of its construction.

There are five basic methods of shoe construction - (1) Goodyear Welt; (2) McKay or Nailed; (3) Cement; (4) Stitchdown; and (5) Hand Turned. The first four are the most popular and are used in the building of men's, women's and children's shoes. The Hand Turned shoe at present is not a popular method of construction and is usually used only in making shoes for elderly women, some types of bedroom slippers and dancing shoes.

The Goodyear Welt type of construction is considered the best for that type of shoe is stronger, wears longer and holds it's shape better.

The McKay or Nailed process is usually used to build cheaper grades of men's and children's shoes. It is also used extensively in the construction of women's shoes.

The Cement process is a variation of the McKay method and is used for the construction of the majority of women's dress type shoes.

The Stitchdown method is used mostly for the construction of children's shoes because of the flexibility it gives.

Practically all shoes, regardless of process, are made over a last. A last is a wooden mold or model of an average human foot for the particular size it is made for. When making shoes a last must be used for each size of shoe. For example, one last is needed for a man's right shoe, size 8-D; another is needed for the left shoe, size 8-D, etc. See Figure 5.

(Figure 5 on Page 10)

(Fig. 5)
Shoe Last

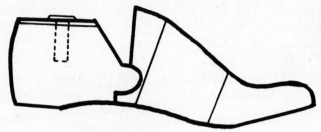

A last is needed for each size, width, and style shoe.

(Fig. 6)

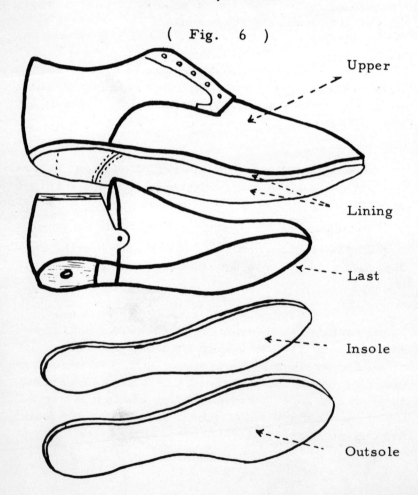

Upper

Lining

Last

Insole

Outsole

(See figure 6 on page 10)

The only difference in the different types or processes of making shoes is the method of fastening the bottom to the upper. In general, the upper parts are cut and sewed together and then slid over the top of the last, the insole tacked to the bottom of the last and the upper then stretched over the last tightly and fastened to the insole.   This is known as LASTING.   The outsole and heel (bottom) are then fastened to the insole. Note Figure 6. The student will note that the insole is the part the foot rests on and is the foundation of the shoe. Before repairing any shoe always check on the inside of it to see what condition the insole may be in.   The insole must be strong enough to hold a new bottom.   If the insole of a worn shoe is badly broken it is not advisable to try to resole or reheel the shoe, for it will not be able to hold the shoe together.

1. - GOODYEAR WELT SHOE.   Briefly, the Goodyear Welt shoe is constructed in the following manner:

A - A rib, or shoulder, is cut and formed on the flesh side of the insole. See Figure 7.

(Fig. 7)
Insole

Shoulder or Rib
on insole.

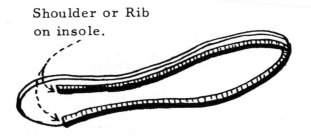

B -   A piece of canvas duck is cemented to the area inside and including the ribs as shown in Figure 8. The canvas is for reinforcement for the rib and serves as a better holding surface for inseam stitches.

(Fig. 8)

Insole

Canvas Duck cemented to Insole

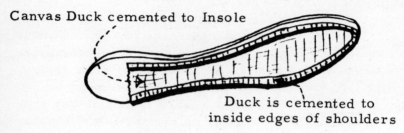

Duck is cemented to inside edges of shoulders

C - The insole is then fastened to the last with the ribbed side out.

D - The upper is then pulled down over the last and tacked temporarily in place on the insole. See Figure 9.

(Fig. 9)

Upper "pulled over" last and tacked to insole prior to lasting and welting.

Last

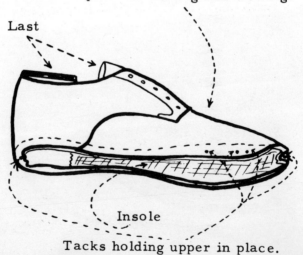

Insole

Tacks holding upper in place.

E - Next a strip of leather known as welting is sewed
with waxed thread to the upper and to the rib of the
insole.   The stitch used in this operation is a chain
stitch and the seam formed by the welt and upper to
the rib is known as the INSEAM. See Figure 10.
Welting is a strip of leather which is usually 4 to 6
iron thick and about a 1/2 inch wide. It is made with
a groove on one side for the stitch of the inseam to
lay in.

(Fig. 10)

Sewing Welt To Shoe

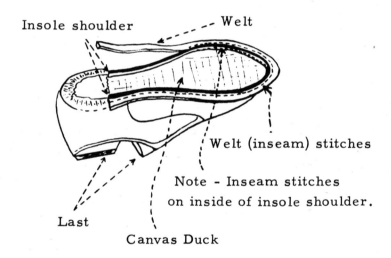

Insole shoulder   -- Welt

Welt (inseam) stitches

Note - Inseam stitches
on inside of insole shoulder.

Last

Canvas Duck

F - The area between the ribs and level with the top
of them is then filled in with either cork or leather
filler.   This makes the bottom perfectly level from
rib to rib. See Figure 11. (Page 14)

G - The bottom or outer sole is then sewed to the
welt with a lock stitch and this seam is known as the
outseam. See Figure 12. (Page 14)

H -   The heel is then nailed on.

(Fig. 11)
Shank Piece
Inserted in shank.

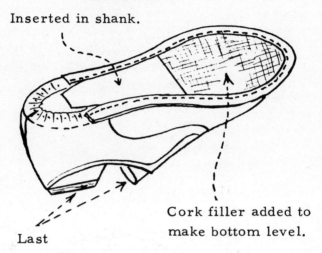

Cork filler added to
make bottom level.

Last

(Fig. 12)
H e e l

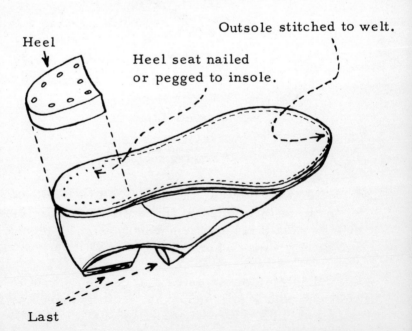

Outsole stitched to welt.

Heel

Heel seat nailed
or pegged to insole.

Last

I - After the heel has been nailed on a heeled pad is put on the inside of the shoe to cover the clinched nails of the heel.   Thus no nails or stitches come in contact with the foot. See Figure 13.

(Fig. 13)

Cutaway of a

Goodyear Welt Shoe

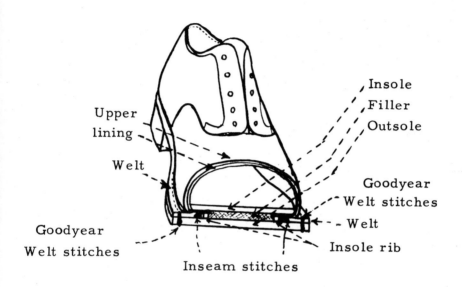

Upper
lining

Welt

Goodyear
Welt stitches

Insole
Filler
Outsole

Goodyear
Welt stitches

Welt

Insole rib

Inseam stitches

2. -   THE MCKAY AND NAILED TYPES.   These shoes are constructed in the following manner: -

A -   After the insole has been properly fitted on the last, the upper is stretched tightly over the last and fastened securely to the underside of the insole by means of tacks. The tacks go through the insole and clinch on the upper side of it.

B -   The outer sole is then fastened on the insole by either stitching or nailing. In either event the stitches

or nails pass through the outer sole, upper and insole. See Figures 14 and 15 below.

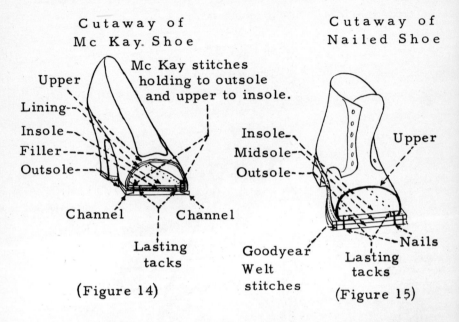

Cutaway of
Mc Kay Shoe

Cutaway of
Nailed Shoe

McKay stitches
holding to outsole
and upper to insole.

Upper

Lining

Insole

Filler

Outsole

Insole

Midsole

Outsole

Upper

Channel   Channel

Lasting
tacks

Goodyear
Welt
stitches

Lasting
tacks

Nails

(Figure 14)

(Figure 15)

C - To insure a smooth surface on the inside of the
shoe the stitches are worked down into the insole and
if nails are used they must be securely clinched .
A thin piece of leather shaped to fit the insole is cemented over the top of the insole insuring a smooth
surface, for the foot to rest on. This piece of leather
is known as a SOCK LINER.

3. - CEMENT PROCESS. Cemented shoes are made by
the following method:

A - This type of shoe is constructed the same way
that McKay shoes are made except that the upper is
cemented to the insole instead of tacked. The cement
used is a Leather Celluloid Cement.

B - The outer sole is then Cemented to the upper
that is lapped over the insole.   Leather Celluloid
is used for this operation. See Figure 16, page 17.

(Fig. 16)

Cutaway of

Cement Shoe

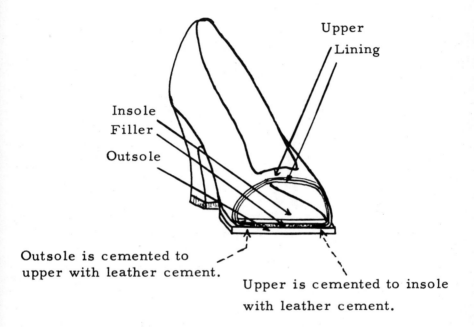

Upper

Lining

Insole

Filler

Outsole

Outsole is cemented to
upper with leather cement.

Upper is cemented to insole
with leather cement.

4. - THE STITCHDOWN PROCESS.

A - This process is used mostly in constructing
children's, boy's, and girl's shoes because of its
greater flexibility;

B - This process differs from all other methods of
construction in that when the upper is pulled over the
last it is not fastened to the underside of the insole.
After the upper has been stretched over the last it is
turned out and stitched down on the out sole. See
Figure 17.

C - A strip of welt is stitched over the upper for re-
enforcement. Note Figure 17, next page.

(Fig. 17)

Cutaway of
Stitchdown Shoe

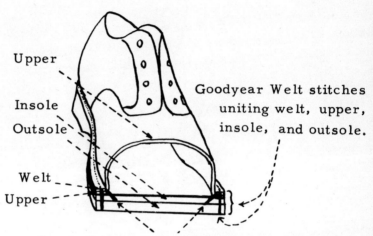

Upper

Insole

Outsole

Welt

Upper

Goodyear Welt stitches
uniting welt, upper,
insole, and outsole.

Stitches holding upper to insole.

5. - HAND TURNED PROCESS.

General: - Even though at the present time this
process is not very popular it is briefly described here so that the student will recognize it.
The Turned Shoe is very difficult to resole and
therefore it is recommended that until the student
becomes a skilled shoe repairmen he ''lay off''
accepting them for repair.   This process gets
it's name from the fact that the upper is lasted
wrong side out, then after lasting, is turned right
side out.   This process makes an exceptionally
flexible shoe which is due to the fact that it has
only one sole.

(Fig. 18)

Cutaway of
Hand-Turned Shoe

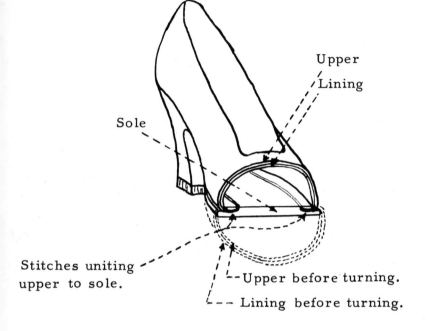

Upper
Lining

Sole

Stitches uniting
upper to sole.

Upper before turning.

Lining before turning.

A - In preparing the out sole, it is cut to the proper size and a shoulder is formed near the edge
and the upper is lasted against it. See Figure 18.

B - A channel is formed in the sole, and the upper
is stitched against the shoulder with the stitches
passing through the upper and then through the sole
to the channel.

C - Next the last is removed and the shoe is turned right side out.

D - The shoe is then relasted by hand.

E -   The heel is attached and the shoe finished off.

F - A SOCK LINER is usually placed on the inside of the shoe to cover the stitches. In order
to identify this process the Sock Liner must be
lifted as usually, from outward appearances the
HAND TURNED shoe is hard to distinguish from
other methods of construction. Study Figure 18
so that the turned shoe can be recognized.

LESSON   IV
SMALL HAND TOOLS WHICH FACILITATE SHOE REPAIRING

In spite of the fact that about 50% of shoe repair
work is done by hand, the operator needs relatively
few types of tools.

It cannot be stressed too strongly that a repairman should use only the best quality of tools and that
they be kept in good condition.

Keep your knives sharp at all times for accurate
cutting cannot be done with a dull or nicked blade. By
the same token it takes twice as long to do a job with
an unsharpened knife. Buy good quality knives and
they will retain their edge better and longer.

Pictured in the following illustrations are some
types of necessary tools and their uses. Different
makes of tools will vary slightly in design but all are
made basically the same for each tool has a definite
purpose and use.

The various machines used in the repair of shoes
will be illustrated as their use comes up.

(Fig. 19)

Hand Tools

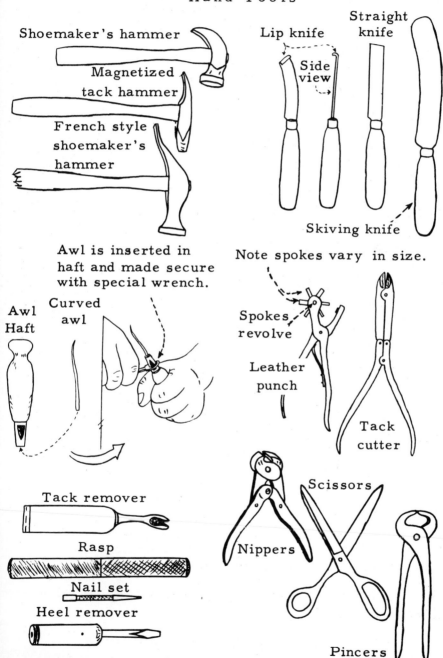

Shoemaker's hammer

Magnetized
tack hammer

French style
shoemaker's
hammer

Lip knife

Straight
knife

Side
view

Skiving knife

Awl is inserted in
haft and made secure
with special wrench.

Note spokes vary in size.

Awl
Haft

Curved
awl

Spokes
revolve

Leather
punch

Tack
cutter

Tack remover

Rasp

Nail set

Heel remover

Scissors

Nippers

Pincers

(Fig. 19)

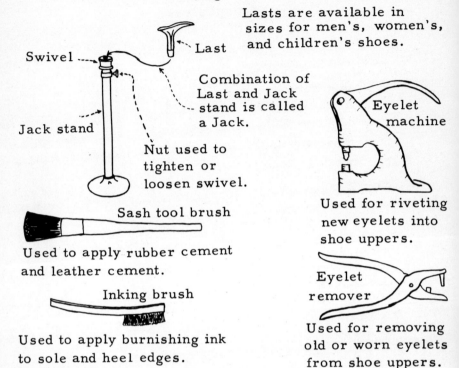

Lasts are available in sizes for men's, women's, and children's shoes.

Swivel

Last

Combination of Last and Jack stand is called a Jack.

Jack stand

Nut used to tighten or loosen swivel.

Eyelet machine

Used for riveting new eyelets into shoe uppers.

Sash tool brush

Used to apply rubber cement and leather cement.

Inking brush

Used to apply burnishing ink to sole and heel edges.

Eyelet remover

Used for removing old or worn eyelets from shoe uppers.

LESSON   V
NAILS COMMONLY USED FOR SHOE REPAIRING

For each type of material and job in shoe repairing there is a specific nail. In the following illustration each type of nail and it's use is shown. Figure 20.

Pegs and nails were used almost exclusively to fasten the bottoms on to shoes long before modern methods of sewing, cementing, etc., were introduced. Today many soles and heels can be attached only by nailing and a certain amount of nailing is required along with sewing and cementing.

Regardless of the type of construction of a shoe it can be resoled by the nailing method.

Although many manufacturers make shoe repair nails the size of the nails are standard. Designs of the various types are as near standard as possible as each nail has a specific use.

(Fig. 20)

Shoe Repair Nails

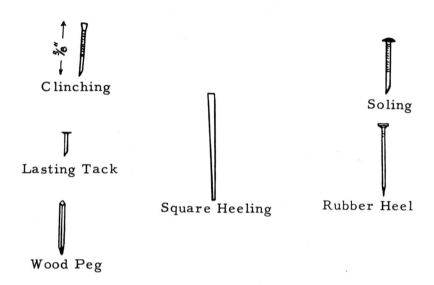

Clinching

Lasting Tack

Wood Peg

Square Heeling

Soling

Rubber Heel

1. - SHOE NAILS and their uses.

A - CLINCHING NAIL - used for nailing leather.

B - SOLING NAIL - used for nailing rubber and chrome leather.

C - SQUARE HEELING NAIL - used for leather heel bases and leather heels.

D - RUBBER HEEL NAIL - used for rubber heels.

E - WOOD HEEL NAIL - used for leather lifts on wood heels.

F - WOOD PEGS - used for pegging and to fill old nail holes.

G - LASTING TACKS - used for lasting and temporary holding.

H-All of the above nails come in various lengths to meet requirements. All of the above except Lasting Tacks are sized by eights of an inch. For example: a 5/8 nail is 5/8 of an inch in length.   The size of Lasting Tacks is denoted by numbers such as 1, 2, 3, 4, etc. The smaller the number the smaller the tack.

2. - Proper Placing of a Nail into a Shoe.

A - The following directions apply to the driving of any type of soling or heeling nail into a shoe.

B - In Figure 20 it will be noted that the points of Clinching and Soling nails differ from ordinary nails in that one side is perfectly straight while the other side curves over to the straight side, thus forming the point. Shoe nails are made in this manner to aid in clinching.

C - Set the nail at a slight angle with the point pointing toward the ball or center of the shoe and with the head tipped back slightly. See Figure 21.

D - Note that the straight edge of the nail is facing the center of the shoe and the curved edge is facing out. Shoe nails <u>must</u> be placed in this manner to insure proper clinching.

Placing of Shoe Nail

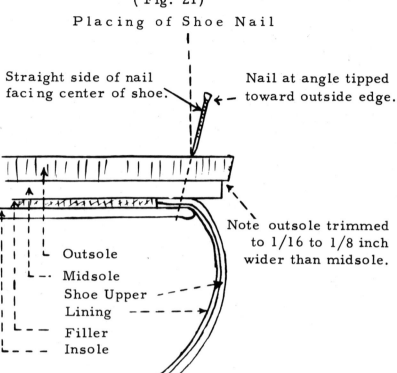

Straight side of nail facing center of shoe.

Nail at angle tipped toward outside edge.

Note outsole trimmed to 1/16 to 1/8 inch wider than midsole.

Outsole
Midsole
Shoe Upper
Lining
Filler
Insole

E -   The length of the nail to be used is determined by the number of layers the nail must penetrate. The nail should be just a trifle longer than the layers to be nailed so that it will strike the last and bend over (clinch). Study Figure 22. (Page 26)

F -   Drive nail in directly - - do not bend nail over on top surface. If nail bends when hit, remove it.

G - Always set nails in neat rows and keep them evenly spaced. Always do neat workmanship.

H - When nailing, hold shoe on last so that each nail, as it is being driven, will strike the last and clinch.

(Fig. 22)

C l i n c h e d   N a i l

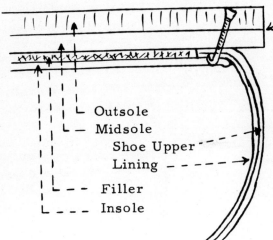

Note that outsole has "pulled in" flush with midsole edge when nail is clinched. See Figure 21.

Outsole
Midsole
Shoe Upper
Lining
Filler
Insole

Note that nail is set so that it holds outsole, midsole, and upper to insole.

I - After nailing shoe always check inside for any nails that may not have clinched. The best way to make enemies of your customers is to leave nails "sticking up" on the inside of the shoe.

LESSON   VI

HOW   TO   PREPARE   SOLES

The first step in resoling shoes is the proper preparation of the top or whole sole to be used. Hard Oak leather must be Tempered.

Tempering leather is the process of softening it so that it will be more flexible and durable. Tempered leather is easier to shape, cut, stitch

and finish. Using Hard Oak leather without tempering may cause it to crack or break while trying to
work it. Leather is tempered by submerging it in
a liquid and then allowing it to MULL.

Liquids used for tempering are water or an
oil made up of a mixture of 90% mineral oil and
10% neatsfoot oil. It is recommended that if water
is used the leather be allowed to soak in it from 4
to 6 minutes. When using the oil mixture submerge
the leather for 10 to 15 minutes. One common
fault is to allow the leather to remain in water too
long. Allowing the leather to remain in water too
long will weaken it as most of the acids necessary
for its durability will be soaked away. Temper -
ing applies only to Oak Leather as Chrome Leather does not need it.

1. - Pre-temper preparation.

A - Skive (bevel) flesh side of tap butt.
(Skiving is described in paragraph #3)

B - Rough up the flesh side of tap on finisher
bottom sanding wheel or with rasp.

C - With sash tool brush (small bristle) apply
a thin coat of rubber cement on entire roughed
surface.   Work cement in thoroughly and
allow cement to dry.

2. - Tempering

A - After above preparations have been made
submerge taps in liquid to be used.   (Water
or oil mixture)

B - When taps have been in liquid the alloted
time, remove them and allow to drain.

(Fig. 23)

Side View of Skived Tap

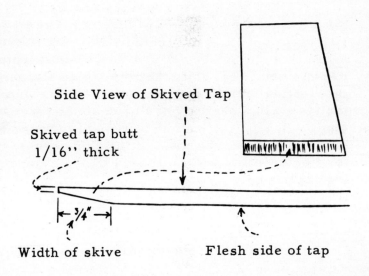

Side View of Skived Tap

Skived tap butt
1/16'' thick

|← ¾'' →|

Width of skive   Flesh side of tap

C - Taps can now be mulled by either one of
two methods.
    (1) Place taps together, grain side to
    grain side and set on edge in a tight,
    damp cabinet or box.
    (2) Wrap taps with either newspapers
    or with damp gunny-sack.

D - Allow taps to mull for at least 12 hours
before using. This amount of time is needed
for the liquid to thoroughly penetrate the leather. Partially soaked leather will not handle
properly.

(Fig. 24)

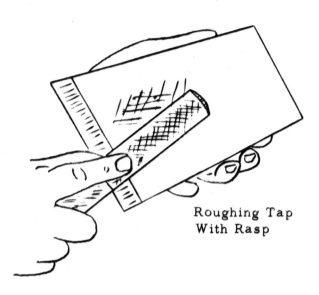

Roughing Tap
With Rasp

E -   Tempered leather can be kept in that
condition indefinitely if left in a damp atmosphere. Because of the time element necessary for tempering several pairs of taps
should be kept prepared ahead at all times.
Figure 25 shows one type of tempering and
mulling cabinet.

F - Leather may be tempered by the above
method without applying the rubber cement.
Applying rubber cement before tempering is
suggested because it will have more holding

power when applied to a dry surface rather than to a damp surface.

G -   Whole, or full soles, are tempered by the same method as described above.

(Fig. 25)

Tempering Cabinet

Cabinet must be made moisture-proof.

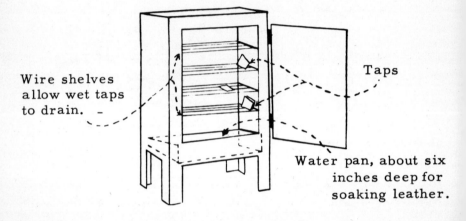

Wire shelves allow wet taps to drain. -

Taps

Water pan, about six inches deep for soaking leather.

3.   Skiving the Tap.

A - The tap is held with the left hand in such manner that it is horizontal to the floor and with the flesh side down.

B - Place the butt of the tap between the two rollers of the machine which has a cutting blade between them. See figure 26.

C - Hold the tap level.

D -   Turn crank of machine with right hand and allow the wheels to feed the tap to the cutting blade. Do not force the sole - - - - merely hold and steer the tap with the left hand.

(Fig. 26)

A   S k i v i n g   M a c h i n e

Rollers

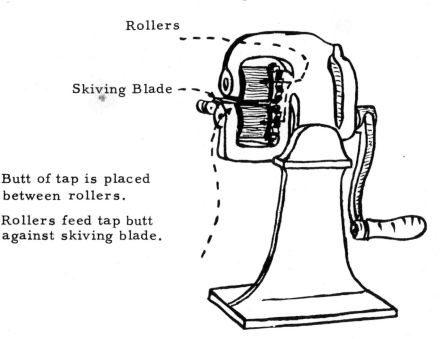

Skiving Blade

Butt of tap is placed
between rollers.

Rollers feed tap butt
against skiving blade.

E - As a rule the skive should be about 3/4 of an inch to an inch in width. The edge of the butt should be about 1/16 of an inch thick when skived. Do not skive the tap butt to a "feather edge". See Figure 27.

F - The cutting blade may be adjusted to make the skive wider or deeper according to the skive desired. To do this a simple screw arrangement is on all makes of machines so that the blade can be lowered or

raised accordingly. A manual is furnished
by the machine manufacturer on the adjust -
ment of the skiving machine - study it thoroughly.

(Fig. 27)

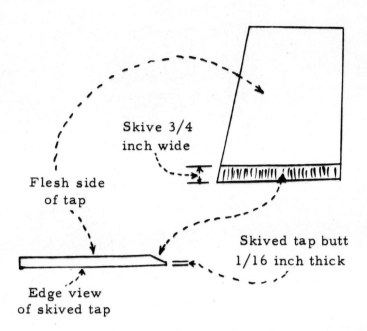

Skive 3/4
inch wide

Flesh side
of tap

Edge view
of skived tap

Skived tap butt
1/16 inch thick

G -Tap butt can be skived with the straight
knife if no machine is available.   Machine
skiving is recommended because of its speed
and accuracy.

(1) Lay tap on work bench, flesh side up
with the butt near bench edge.

(2) Hold tap with left hand and with straight
knife in right hand skive tap butt. See Figure
28, next page.

(Fig. 28)

Skiving Tap By Hand

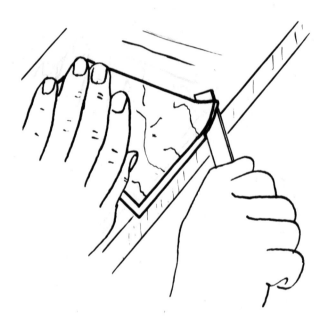

LESSON   VII

HOW TO RESOLE MEN'S GOODYEAR WELT
SINGLE SOLED SHOE

Before going further study Figures 29 and 30 thoroughly so that you will know all parts and sections of a shoe. The parts and sections as shown there are the same on every shoe regardless of style, kind, or type of construction.

(Figures 29 and 30)

The Parts Of A Shoe

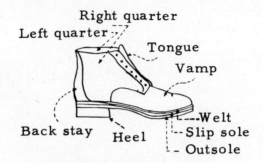

Right quarter
Left quarter
Tongue
Vamp
Welt
Slip sole
Back stay   Heel   Outsole

Cutaway of Shoe

Quarter   Eyelet
Counter   Eyelet facing
Vamp
Back stay   Insole
Welt
Heel   Steel   Insole
shank   Slip sole
Heel pad   Outsole

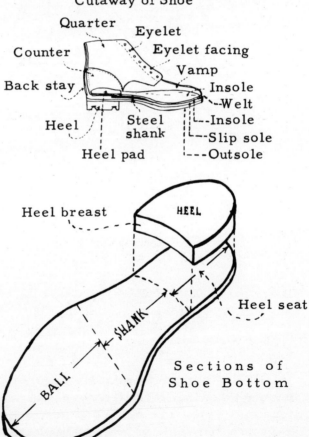

Heel breast   HEEL

Heel seat

SHANK

BALL

Sections of
Shoe Bottom

1. - NAILED SHANK

A - Select the size and thickness of taps required
for the pair of shoes to be repaired.   Select taps
of the approximate thickness of the soles that were
originally on the shoe.   As a guide, man's dress
shoes usually are made with 7 to 9 iron soles and
work shoes with 10 to 12 iron soles.   Remember
to use only tempered taps.

B - Place the shoe on the last with the sole up.
See Figure 31.

(Fig. 31)

Placing Shoe on Last

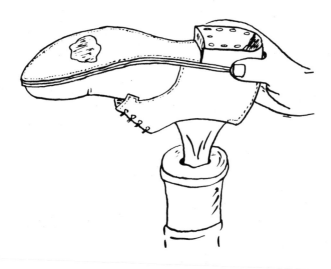

C - A new half sole should be one half the length
of the shoe. This is measured from the front edge
of the toe back to the back of the heel seat through
the center of the shoe. See Figure 32, page 36.

Tap is placed on shoe bottom
at an angle - the outside corner
being about 1/4 inch closer to the
heel breast than the inside corner.

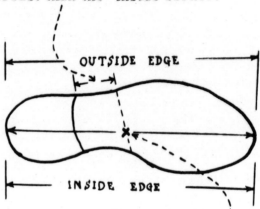

1/2 sole (tap) is placed on shoe
bottom half way between the back
of the heel seat and the toe.

D - Place the tap on the shoe, grain side up, so
that the butt of the tap, on the center point, is at
an angle.   The outside corner of the tap butt,
should be about 1/4 inch closer to the heel breast
than the inside corner. See Figures 32 and 33.

NOTE: A half sole is always placed on the shank at an
angle so that it will conform to the bend of the shoe
in walking. Putting the tap straight across the shank
will tend to make the shoe stiff and will break the shoe
across the shank.

E - Hold the tap in place and with the back corner of the straight knife draw a line across the
shank of the shoe. The butt of the tap is to be put
in place along this line. See Figure 34.

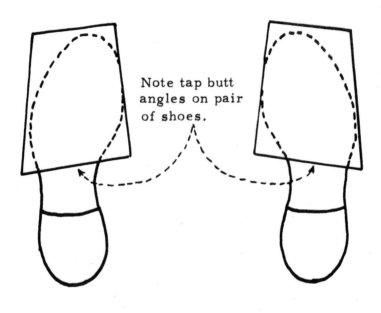

Note tap butt
angles on pair
of shoes.

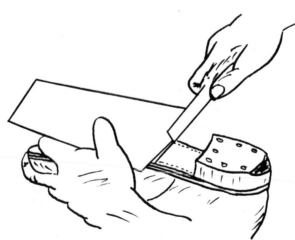

With aid of tap draw
a line across the shank
as per Figure 32.

(Fig. 35)

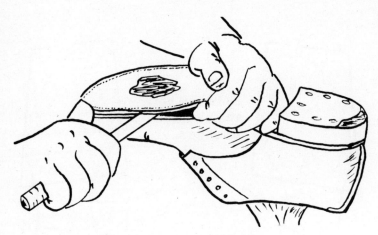

Cutting worn sole from
welt with straight knife.

F - Remove the tap. Insert the front point of the
straight knife between the outer sole and the welt
at a point about 3/4 inch ahead of the line drawn
on the shank. See Figure 35. Proceed to cut the
old stitches all the way around the shoe to a point
about 3/4 inch ahead of the shank line on the opposite side of the shoe.

G - Cut the old sole off about one inch above the
line drawn across the shank. This is known as
"butting the sole" . See Figure 36.

H - With the straight knife, or skiving knife, skive
the shank of the shoe from the shank line down to
a feather edge.   Make the skive about 3/4 inch
wide, thus the skived butt of the tap will fit properly on the skived part of the shank of the shoe,
forming a perfect joint. See Figures 37 and 38.

I - Next inspect the filler. If pieces of the filler
are missing replace with tar-felt or cork. Fit

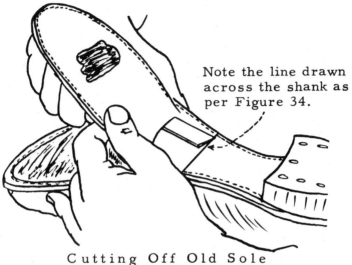

Note the line drawn
across the shank as
per Figure 34.

Cutting Off Old Sole
Known As ''Butting''

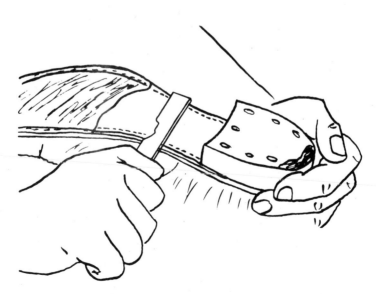

Skiving Shoe Shank

replacements in filler so that there are no
bumps - remember filler must be level and
smooth.   Cement filler replacements in place
with rubber cement.   If there are any bumps in
the filler skive them off so that the bottom of the
shoe is level.   If there is any filler or foreign
substance on the welt, clean it off thoroughly.

(Fig. 38)

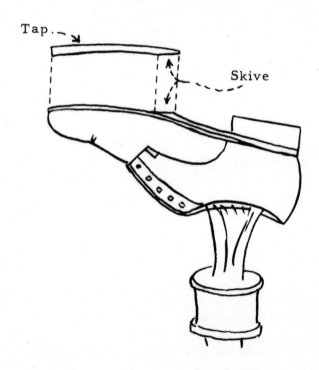

J - Remove the old stitches from the top side of
the welt with a stitch removing machine or by
hand with an awl.   This is done because if the
old stitches are allowed to remain in the welt
they will work loose in time and give an unsightly
appearance to your job. Also the welt will last

longer and the shoe can be resoled oftener if
old stitches are removed each time.

K - Next check the inseam (stitches holding
welt and upper to shoulder of insole). If it is
loose in a place or two reinforce it with a
few lasting tacks. Use tacks that are just long
enough to go thru welt, upper and thru the insole
and clinch. If the welt is worn or broken in
places, replace where necessary. Rewelting is
described in Lesson 24.

L - Now rough up the bottom of the welt and
the skived shank with a rasp or on the bottom sanding wheel of the finisher. See Figure
39. Remember just rough the skive and the welt
lightly so that the rubber cement will have a
holding surface.

M - Brush on a thin coat of rubber cement on
bottom of shoe - skive to toe. Brush cement on
evenly and work into surface. See Figure 40.
Allow cement to dry.

N - Apply a thin coat of rubber cement to flesh
side of tap. Allow to dry. See Figure 40.

NOTE: - When using rubber cement always rough
up both surfaces to be cemented. Surfaces are
roughed so that cement will have a holding surface.
Rubber cement will not hold as well when applied to
a smooth surface. Spread a thin coat of cement on
both surfaces and allow to dry normally. After the
cement on both surfaces has dried place the two cemented surfaces together. Then tap lightly so that
cement on the two surfaces will fuse.

O - After cement on tap has dried, mould it by
grasping the opposite edges with both hands and

Roughing Skive and Welt With Rasp

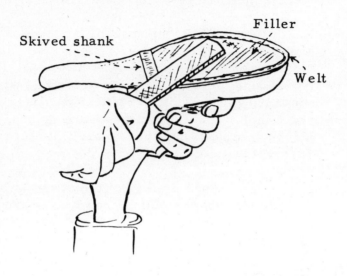

Skived shank

Filler

Welt

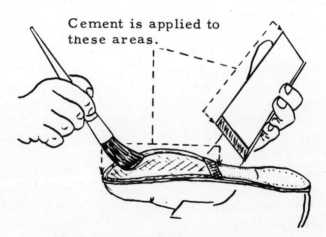

Cement is applied to these areas.

Applying Rubber Cement To Shoe
Bottom and Tap With Sash Tool Brush

bending edges toward each other.   Flesh side of the tap is held up.   Then grasp butt and toe end and bend down. This will give tap a rounded shape and it will conform with curvature of shoe bottom.

P -   Place the butt of tap (flesh side down) on the skived part of the shank.   When properly placed round the joint with hammer. Next lay tap down on the shoe - from butt to toe.   Be sure the tap covers the surface of the shoe completely.   See Figure 41.   Pound the tap lightly over entire surface so that tap and shoe bottom are thoroughly cemented together.

(Fig. 41)

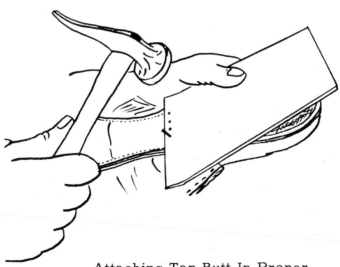

Attaching Tap Butt In Proper
Position On Shoe Shank. Butt
Skive Joined To Shank Skive.

(Fig. 42)

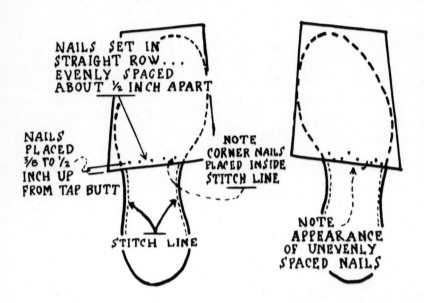

NAILS SET IN STRAIGHT ROW... EVENLY SPACED ABOUT ½ INCH APART

NAILS PLACED ⅜ TO ½ INCH UP FROM TAP BUTT

NOTE CORNER NAILS PLACED INSIDE STITCH LINE

STITCH LINE

NOTE APPEARANCE OF UNEVENLY SPACED NAILS

Q - Next nail the butt of the tap to the shank of the shoe with Clinching Nails. 4 1/2/8 to 5/8 nails are usually used on men's dress shoes and 5/8 to 6/8 nails used on work shoes. A row of nails is placed parallel to the butt of the tap and about 1/4 of an inch up from the butt. See Figure 41. The nails should be placed about 3/8 to 1/2 inch apart. The nails on each side should be placed on the inside of the stitch line so that the sole can be stitched without striking nails. In placing the nails keep them in a straight line and all evenly spaced. See Figure 42.

R - If the shoes to be repaired are to have new rubber heels remove the old heel at this time. If the old heel is all leather and is to be entirely replaced, remove it.

S -   After old heel has been removed fill old nail holes with wood pegs.

NOTE: Directions for heel removing and reheeling will be given in a separate chapter.

T - Now remove the shoe from the last and prepare to trim the excess leather off the tap.

U - Grasp the shoe with the left hand, the bottom of the shoe facing down and with the toe of the shoe against the operator's chest. See Figure 43.

(Fig. 43)

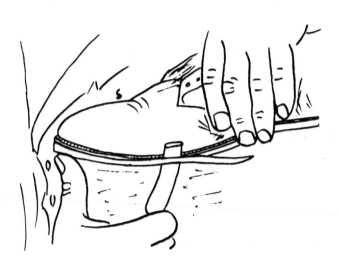

Trimming Sole Edge With Lip Knife.

Note the use of the thumb as a lever.

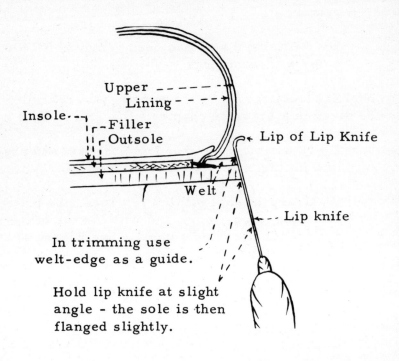

Upper

Lining

Insole

Filler

Outsole

Lip of Lip Knife

Welt

Lip knife

In trimming use
welt-edge as a guide.

Hold lip knife at slight
angle - the sole is then
flanged slightly.

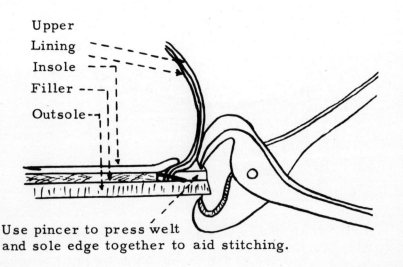

Upper

Lining

Insole

Filler

Outsole

Use pincer to press welt
and sole edge together to aid stitching.

V -   Take the right-handed lip-knife in the right hand and starting at the butt of the tap cut off the excess leather protruding past the welt edge.

W -   Hold the knife in the palm of the hand, keep the thumb on the tap edge ahead of the knife blade and let it act as a lever. See Figure 43.

X - Trim toward your body and as you near the toe part of the shoe turn the shoe around.   Therefore when trimming the opposite edge the heel of the shoe is braced against the chest.

Y - Trim the tap flush with the welt.

Z -   When trimming hold the knife in such a way that the back side of the knife "slides" on the welt as a guide. Hold the handle out so that the edge of tap is flanged out slightly. See Figure 44.

A-1- Now take pincer and lightly, but firmly, pinch the welt flat to the tap to insure a tight joint all the way around. See Figure 45.

B-1- The butt of the tap has caused a slight ridge across the shank. Smooth off this ridge on the bottom sanding wheel of the finisher. See Figure 46. Bottom sanding is described in a separate chapter.

C-1- When resoling the above shoe with a rubber or chrome tap the same procedure is followed but with one exception. When attaching either a rubber or chrome tap, Soling Nails instead of Clinching Nails are used. It is advisable to place two rows of alternately spaced nails across the butt of rubber and chrome tap. See Figure 47.

(Fig. 46)

Shanks Before And After Scouring

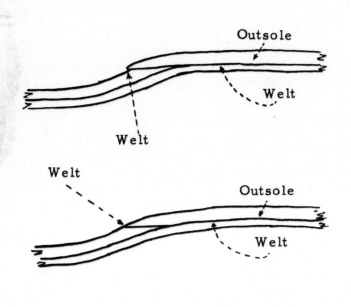

(Fig. 47)

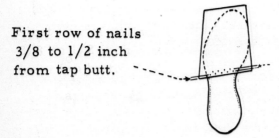

First row of nails
3/8 to 1/2 inch
from tap butt.

Second row of nails
alternately spaced
and 3/8 to 1/2 inch
above the first row.

D-1- The sole is now ready to be stitched to the welt.

E-1- When repairing shoes always work both shoes of the pair at the same time. As the two shoes are mates, do them both alike so that they will still look like mates when they are repaired.   Be sure that the butts of the taps are the same distance from the heel breasts and that the angles on both are the same. See Figure 48.

(Fig. 48)

Repaired Shoes Of Pair
Must Look Like Mates

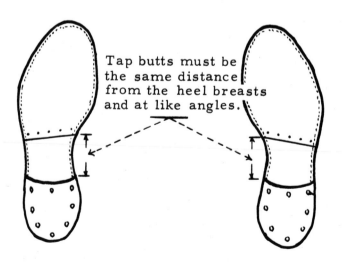

Tap butts must be the same distance from the heel breasts and at like angles.

LESSON   VIII

HOW THE CURVED NEEDLE STITCHER IS OPERATED

There are on the market both Curved Needle and Straight Needle stitching machines for sewing soles on Goodyear Welt shoes.   The machines get their names from the fact that one type uses a curved needle and awl; and the other uses a straight needle and awl. See Figure 49.

(Figure 49)

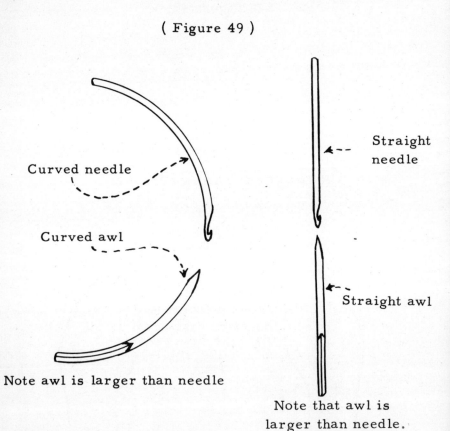

Curved needle

Curved awl

Straight needle

Straight awl

Note awl is larger than needle

Note that awl is larger than needle.

The curved needle machines are the more popular and most shoe repairmen are of the opinion that the curved needle machine is more convenient for repair work. Because of that fact, the operations of the curved needle machine will be given here.

(Figure 50)

Goodyear Outsole Rapid Lockstitch Machine - Model E

"B" indicates
work table

"A" indicates
presser foot

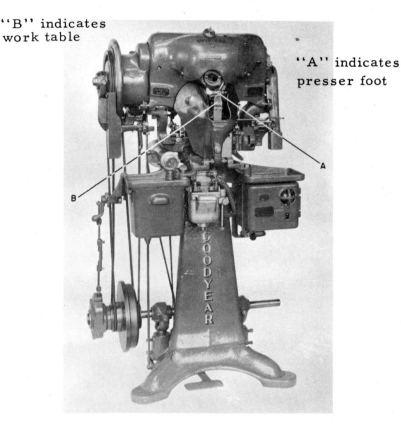

The principles of all makes of curved needle machines are the same but some adjustments may differ ,
therefore we will give you general adjustments that
are common to all.   A Manual is furnished with each
machine in which threading procedures and all adjustments are given thoroughly.

The operation of all makes of curved needle machines are the same.

Figure 50 illustrates one model of curved needle
stitching machine.   All other types and models are
similar in outward appearances.

(Fig. 51)

Placing Shoe In Stitcher

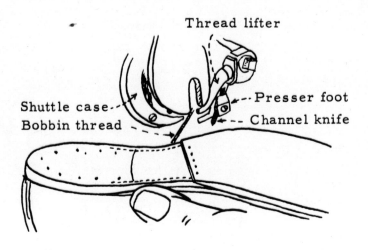

(Fig. 52)

If the heel is on the
shoe, start stitching
as far as possible in
back of the tap butt.

If the heel is on the
shoe, end stitching
as far as possible in
back of the tap butt.

Start stitching at
the beginning of
the welting if the
heel is removed.

End stitching at the
end of the welting if
the heel is off the shoe.

A curved needle sole stitching machine is very
similar to an ordinary sewing machine in that two threads
are employed to tie a knot or stitch, in the material.
The curved needle stitcher employs thread in a bobbin

and thread through the machine. The main difference
between this machine and an ordinary sewing machine
is that the sole stitcher uses an awl to pierce a hole
in the material for the needle to go through.   Other-
wise when operating either machine one is merely
making a seam by sewing two or more pieces of material together.

When stitching leather taps the Channel Knife on
the machine is set just deep enough so that when the
stitch is tied the top of it will be just below the surface of the tap.   A Channel Knife is a small blade
attached to the Presser Foot which cuts a groove or
channel in the tap.   The stitch is tied in the channel.
See Figure 51.

The Channel Knife is not used when stitching rubber taps as a properly tied stitch will pull down into
the rubber and channeling is not necessary.

For the best results use linen stitcher thread in
the machine and bobbin.

The size of the thread to be used is determined
by the type of shoe and soles to be stitched.

1 - Men's dress shoes, to be soled with leather, use
7 cord thread in machine and 6 cord in bobbin.

2 - Men's heavy shoes, double soled, and resoled
with either leather or rubber, use 9 cord in machine
and 8 cord in bobbin.

3 - Ladies and childrens shoes, resoled with leather
or rubber, use 9 cord in machine and 8 cord in bobbin.

Use size needle and awl to fit size of thread being
used. The awl should always be two sizes larger than
needle. Manufacturer's Manual will give proper size

of needle and awl to use with each size thread. Needle and awl sizes are not listed here as different makes of needles and awls do not have standard size identifications. Thread size identifications are standard.

The machine should be set to vary the number of stitches per inch according to type of shoe and material used.

Set the machine so that stitches will go into the original stitch holes on the welt. As a rule they are:

1 - Men's dress shoes - - about 8 stitches per inch.

2 - Men's heavy shoes - - about 6 per inch on leather tap and 5 per inch for rubber tap.

3 - Ladies and children's shoes - - 9 to 10 per inch.

1 - Preparation of Stitcher for Operation.

A - Oil all moving parts thoroughly at least twice a day when in use. Use only high grade lubricants for the stitcher is a precision instrument.   Giving the machine conscientious care and maintenance will insure lifetime service.

B - Fill the wax pot with stitching wax. Check wax pot occasionally while in use and do not allow it to become less than half full at any time. Wax pot should be thoroughly cleaned occasionally as sediment or burned wax in the pot will cause thread breakage.

C - Turn on heating elements. Stitcher must be thoroughly warmed to insure efficient operation when cake wax is used.   When using liquid wax, heating stitcher is not necessary.

D - Place welt of shoe on needle Plate so that heel of shoe is under Shuttle Case.

E -   Try to start the stitches in back of the tap butt
so that the corners of the tap are made secure. See
Figure 52.

NOTE: - It will be noted that the stitching operation
starts at the tap butt on the Outside shank of the Right
Shoe and on the Inside shank of the Left Shoe.   See
Figure 53.

(Figure 53)

Start Stitching On Left Side Edge Of Shoe
Shoe bottom facing operator

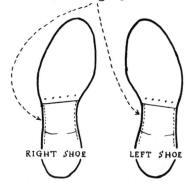

RIGHT SHOE   LEFT SHOE

F - Make sure that the outer edge of the welt is **against**
the shoe guide, or lip of work table. See Figure 54.

(Figure 54)

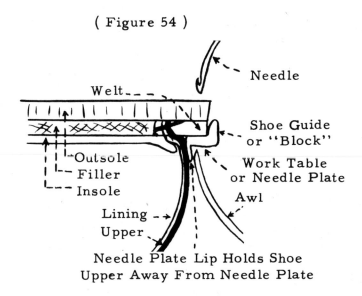

Needle

Welt

Shoe Guide
or "Block"

Outsole
Filler
Insole

Work Table
or Needle Plate

Awl

Lining
Upper

Needle Plate Lip Holds Shoe
Upper Away From Needle Plate

G -   Release the presser foot making sure it holds the shoe firmly.

H - With right hand turn the fly wheel until the awl pierces through the sole. See Figure 55. Remember the shoe is being held by the left hand in original position.

(Figure 55)

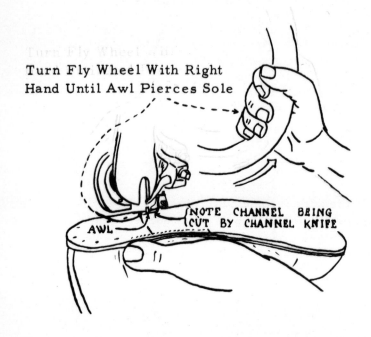

Turn Fly Wheel With Right Hand Until Awl Pierces Sole

AWL

NOTE CHANNEL BEING CUT BY CHANNEL KNIFE

I - The shoe is now ready to be stitched.   Grasp the toe of the shoe with the right hand and the heel and counter of shoe with the left hand.   See Figure 56.   Press the Foot Clutch Pedal with the left foot and the machine will start to stitch.   The speed of the machine is regulated by the amount of pressure applied to the Clutch Pedal.

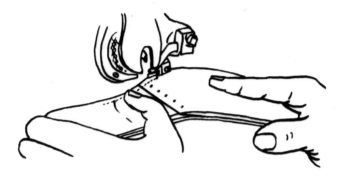

Position Of Hands When
Stitcher Put In Motion

Position Of Hands When Stitching
Around Toe Of Shoe

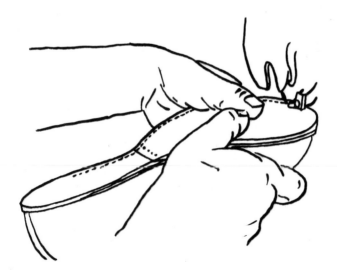

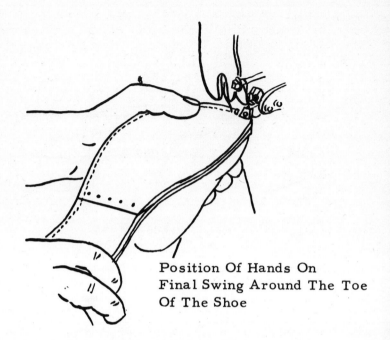

Position Of Hands On
Final Swing Around The Toe
Of The Shoe

Position Of Hands When
Stitching Down Side After
Toe Has Been Rounded

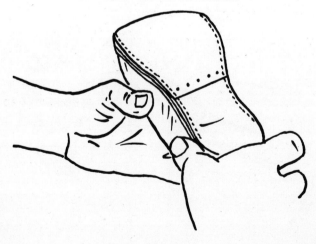

J - As the toe of the shoe is neared, slow down the machine. As the curve of the toe approaches, turn the shoe so that the welt lays on the work table at all times. In other words "steer" the shoe around while stitching.   Do not "run off" the table, the stitching must be one continuous line around the shoe. To "Steer" the shoe around the toe move the left hand to the left side of the shoe, the right hand to the right side of the shoe. The hands are moved while the machine is stitching around the toe. See Figure 57.

K - As stitching progresses around the toe move the right hand to the heel of the shoe.   See Figure 58. In this manner continue to hold shoe firmly on the work table until the tap has been completely stitched . See Figure 58 and 59 .

LESSON   IX
HOW TO KEEP THE STITCHER IN CONDITION

1 - Precautions for the Stitcher Operator.

A - All the operator has to do is put the shoe in the machine, hold the shoe level, guide or steer the shoe and let the machine do the work of "feeding" the shoe and the stitching.

B - Do Not force or push the shoe, the result will be a longer stitch than the machine is set for. It will also result in the bending or breaking of needles and awls.

C - Do Not twist the shoe in the machine - - hold the shoe level at all times.

D - Do Not hold the shoe back from machine feeding . Stitches will be crowded.

E - It is suggested that the student practice stitching on a single piece of leather until he has the "feel" of the machine and has mastered stitching around curves. Do not attempt to stitch a shoe until practice stitching has been mastered.

2 - Precautions Against Needle Breakage.

A - Always use an awl two sizes larger than the needle.

B - Always use the correct size needle for the size thread being used.

C - Never use bent or burred awls. A burred awl is one that has small nicks or breaks on the point.

3 - Common Causes of Thread Breakage.

A - Dirty machine. All parts and rollers must move freely at all times.

B - Improper adjustment of needle, looper, or lifter.

C - Sharp edges or burrs on worn looper, lifter or work table.

D - Auxiliary take-up not working properly.

E - Pulling lock of the stitch too deep. The lock of the stitch should lay from a 1/3 to 1/2 the thickness of the tap. To test the lock of the stitch, sew a few stitches in a single piece of leather. Cut the piece of leather through the stitches (exposing sample stitches) and check the lock of the stitch. See Figure 60.

F - Using dried up bobbin thread.

G - Burned wax in wax pot.

(Figure 60)

Cutaway of Stitches
In Leather

Properly locked stitch should
be locked 1/3 to 1/2 distance of
thickness of the material.

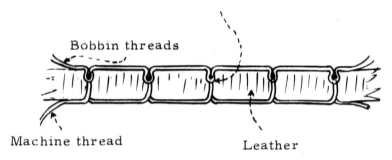

Bobbin threads

Machine thread

Leather

H - Stitching before the machine is properly heated
when using cake wax.

4 - Cleaning Stitcher.

A - Always clean stitcher thoroughly at the end of each
half working day when it is in operation.

B - Keep all rollers, work table, lifter and looper free
of wax at all times.

C - Kerosine or turpentine are recommended as cleaning agents for the stitcher. Do not use gasoline.

D - Use a sash tool brush to apply the cleaning agent
then use cloth to wipe off machine.

5 - Lubrication of Stitcher

A - Machine should be oiled thoroughly before starting operation each half day.

B - Shuttle, all rollers and feed slide must be oiled , during operation.

C - Use only the highest grades of lubricants. Manufacturers Manual will recommend what weight lubricants to use on individual machines.

D - With careful operation, proper lubrications and thorough cleanliness of machine a stitcher will last indefinitely.

LESSON   X

FUNCTIONS OF THE SHOE FINISHING MACHINE

The finishing machine is almost the most important machine to shoe repairing. Regardless of how good a job is done in jacking or stitching the shoe, if it is not finished off so that it has a "like new" appearance, the face value of the job is practically nil.

Repeat sales are made mostly on the appearance of the finished repair job.

Neat finishing requires carefulness and patience.

The Finishing Machines are made up of four sections:

1. Edge Trimmer.
2. Sander .
3. Burnisher.
4. Blower.

(Figure 61.)

Enclosed or Streamlined Finisher Line

"A" - Burnishing   "B" - Sanding   "C" - Edge
      Section   Section   Trimmer Section

"D" - Blower and Dust Collector

Finisher and Curved Needle Stitcher Line

"C" - Blower and Dust Collector Section

"A" -
One
Model
Stitcher

"E" -   "D" -   "B" - Edge
Burnishing   Sanding   Trimmer
Section   Section   Section

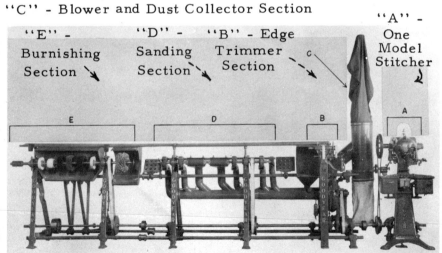

Figure 61 illustrates one model of a complete Finisher line.

Finishers vary in size and number of attachments but all have the same basic wheels and brushes that will be described in succeeding chapters.

1 -   The Edge Trimmer is used for the trimming of the edges of all soles.

2 - The Sander is used for sanding the edges and breast of heels and for scouring and roughing of shoe bottom.

3 -   The Burnisher is used to edge and set the sole edge and to wax and polish sole and heel edges and sole bottoms.

NOTE: -   The operation of the above three sections will be given in separate chapters.

4 -   The Blower consists of a fan that sucks the sander and trimmer dust from the wheels and blows it into a Dust Collector.

5 - Care and Maintenance of Finisher.

A -   Entire Finisher Line should be oiled thoroughly at least twice a day.   Use only the highest grade of lubricants.

    Manufacturer's manual will recommend weight of oil to use. Motor should be oiled frequently while machine is in operation.

B -   Clean entire finisher thoroughly at least once a day. Use a cloth to wipe off finisher dust and kerosene or turpentine to clean off burnishing ink and wax.

C - Empty Dust Collector at least once a day.

D - Be sure that all wheels are locked before starting machine.

E - Do not operate machine with worn or torn sand papers or burnishing wheel covers.

F - Replacing sand paper on heel sanding wheels.

(1) All sanding wheels on the finisher are made of wood with felt base which is covered with sandpaper. See Figure 62 below.

(Figure 62)

Side View Of Sanding Wheel

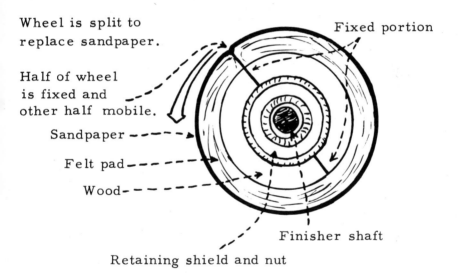

Wheel is split to
replace sandpaper.

Fixed portion

Half of wheel
is fixed and
other half mobile.

Sandpaper

Felt pad

Wood

Finisher shaft

Retaining shield and nut

All wheels are made so that they split open to allow replacement of paper. On both sides of the split are pins to hold the sand paper in place. See Figure 63.

Open sanding wheel and remove old sandpaper. See Figure 63, next page.

(2) Measure off new sandpaper (which comes in

rolls) using old sandpaper as guide.   See Figure 64.

(Figure 63)

Open Sanding Wheel

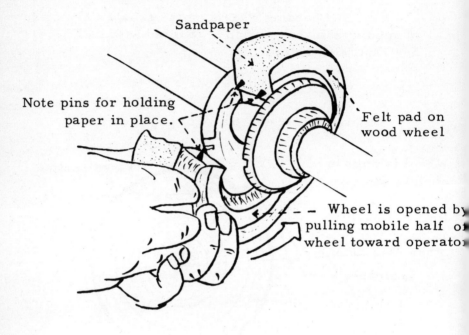

Sandpaper

Note pins for holding
      paper in place.

Felt pad on
wood wheel

Wheel is opened by
pulling mobile half of
wheel toward operator

(Figure 64)

Use removed sandpaper to
measure proper length for
new sandpaper.

Roll of new sandpaper.

Removed sandpaper

Fasten New Paper On
Pegs Opposite Operator

Stretch paper around wheel as
shown and fasten on open end.

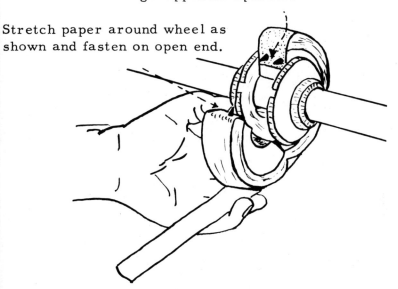

New paper must be
tight on wheels

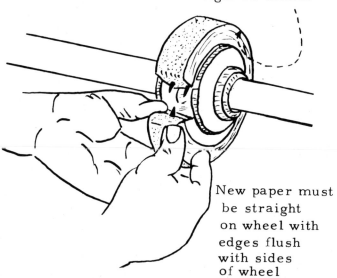

New paper must
be straight
on wheel with
edges flush
with sides
of wheel

(3) Fasten sandpaper on one end of wheel. See Figure 65.

(4) Draw sand paper tightly around wheel. See Figure 66.

(5) Close and lock wheel. See Figure 67.

(Figure 67)

After paper has been properly placed and securely fastened, close wheel by pushing mobile portion away from operator.

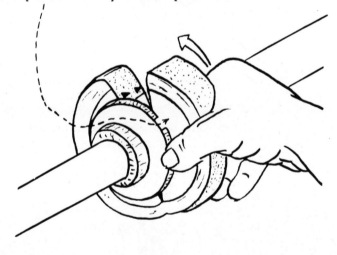

G - Bottom sanding wheel paper is replaced in the same manner as described above. The only exception is the bottom sanding paper comes in sheets the correct size of wheel.

H - Paper for the heel breaster come in pieces shaped like a crescent. See Figure 68 below.

(Figure 68)

Heel Breaster Sandpaper

(1) To replace breaster paper merely unscrew
nut at base of breaster. See Figure 69.

(2) Remove old breaster paper.

(3) Shape breaster paper around breaster wheel
with small part of the crescent at the nut. See Figure
69.

(4) After paper is wrapped around wheel,screw
nut up tight. Nut holds paper in place.

I - Replacing Burnishing Wheel Cover.

(1) Burnishing wheels are made of a wood with a
ribbed rubber base which in turn is covered with a

Burnishing Cloth.   When replacing burnishing cloths
(wheel cover) they <u>must</u> be put on tight.

(Figure 69)

Heel Breaster

To replace breaster paper
loosen retaining nut by turning
it toward the operator. Wrap
the breaster paper around the
wheel (short edge of paper
around small part of wheel).
When the paper is in place,
tighten the retaining nut.
The retaining nut only holds
the paper on the wheel.

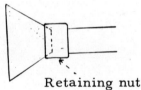

Retaining nut

(2) With special wrench loosen retaining nut on
right side of burnishing wheel. See Figure 70. Remove
old cover.

(3) Place loop of new cover between rubber ribs
and pull cover over wheel away from operator.   See
Figure 71.

(4) Proceed to bring cover around wheel.   Be
sure that cover is pulled tightly.   See Figure 72 and
73.

Loosen retaining nut with burnishing
wheel wrench...turn toward operator.

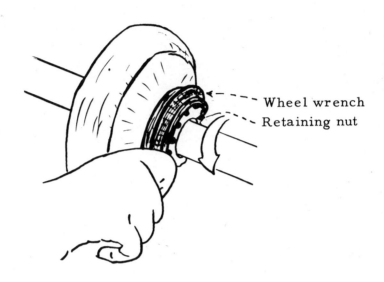

Wheel wrench
Retaining nut

Wood base

Ribbed rubber

Place cover loop-string
between rubber ribs and
begin to stretch cover
around wheel.

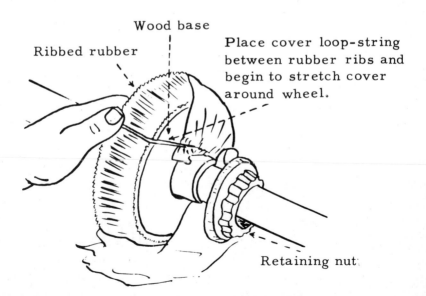

Retaining nut

Ribbed rubber surface

Wheel cover
loop string

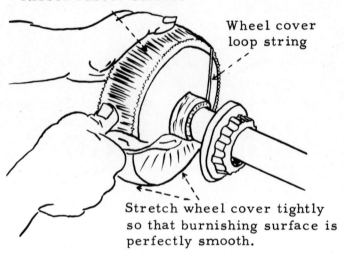

Stretch wheel cover tightly
so that burnishing surface is
perfectly smooth.

Wheel cover is stretched tightly
"bit by bit" around the wheel
insuring a perfectly smooth
burnishing surface.

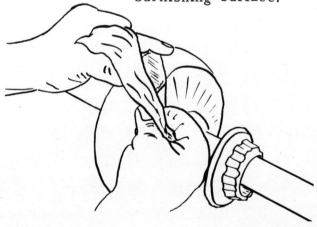

(5)   After cover has been brought completely
around wheel tighten retaining nut.   Note that nut
covers edge of wheel cover and holds it in place.
Turn nut as tightly as possible. See Figure 74.

(Figure 74)

To secure wheel cover, tighten the
retaining nut with a wheel wrench, turn
the nut toward the operator...the cover
is held in place by a retaining nut.

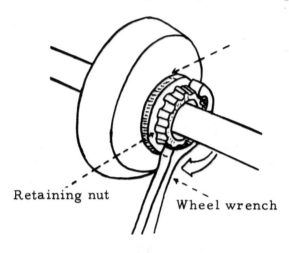

Retaining nut   Wheel wrench

(6)   Apply burnishing ink to top surface of
new wheel cover. Apply brown ink to one of the burnishing wheels and black ink to the other. Burnishing
ink is applied to the new wheel cover for two reasons:
First, it gives a better base for the burnishing wax,
and second, it lengthens the life of the cover.   See
Figure 75.

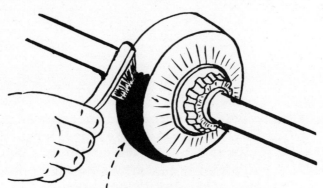

Apply burnishing ink to entire
surface of burnishing wheel.

Apply burnishing wax to the
entire top surface of the
burnishing wheel.

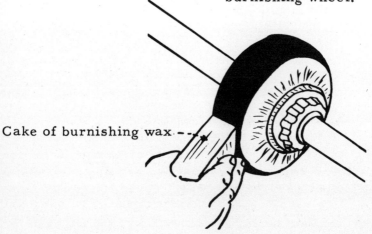

Cake of burnishing wax

(7)After ink has dried apply corresponding color of burnishing wax to wheel surface. See Figure 76.

LESSON XI
HOW THE EDGE TRIMMER IS OPERATED

(Figure 77)

Close-up of edge trimmer

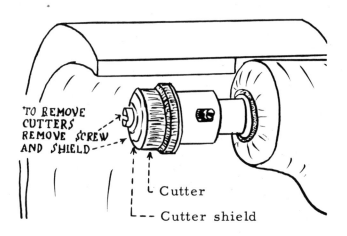

TO REMOVE CUTTERS REMOVE SCREW AND SHIELD

Cutter

Cutter shield

The edge trimmer is used to trim the edges of all soles. After the operation of it has been mastered the operator will be able to finish a sole edge so that it has a factory appearance. The trimmer blades on a shoe repair trimmer are the same as those on a factory trimmer.

The cutter used for sole trimming is a small wheel like tool about 2 1/2 inches in diameter and has 16 tooth like blades. See Figure 78.

A different width cutter is used for each thickness of sole edge. The width of each cutter is measured in

Irons the same as leather.   For a guide as to what
size cutter should be used figure the thickness of welt
plus the thickness of tap. For example: The average
thickness of welt used on men's dress shoes is 5 to
6 irons. The usual thickness of tap used for resoling
this type of shoe is 7 to 9 irons. The total of a 5 iron
welt plus a 7 iron tap is 12 irons, therefore a 12 iron
cutter would be used to trim edge. The size of cutters
regardless of make is standard.

The blades of the cutter must have keen edges at
all times to insure smooth and fast trimming.   The
cutter must be sharpened very frequently but if blades
are sharpened properly they will give long and efficient service. See Figure 79.

(Figure 78)
Edge Trimmer Cutter

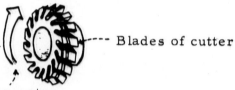

- - - - Blades of cutter

Cutter turns toward operator

(Figure 79)
Trimmer Cutter

Face of blade that
is sharpened.

Proper sharpening gives
the cutter maximum life.

New cutter end view

Note ... Face of blades is ground straight.

All makes of trimmer sections have a cutter sharpening attachment but as each type of attachment differs
it is impossible to give complete directions for sharpening.   However, each attachment is made up of a post
for the cutter to rest on for sharpening operations. The
emery wheels used to sharpen the cutter are standard.
See Figure 80 below.

(Figure 80)

Grinding Surface Must Be Trued At All
Times To Insure Proper Sharpening

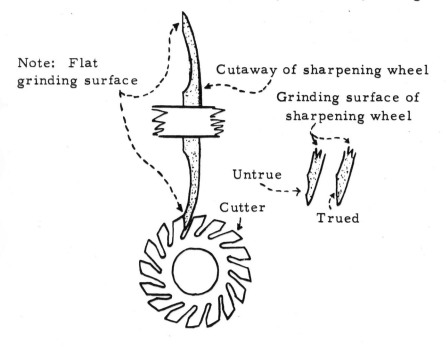

Note: Flat
grinding surface

Cutaway of sharpening wheel

Grinding surface of
sharpening wheel

Untrue

Cutter

Trued

1.   Sharpening Cutter.

A - Adjust post so that the flat, or cutting edge of individual blade is parallel with flat side of emery wheel.
See Figure 80.   Post must also be set so that angled
side of emery wheel will not touch opposite blade. See
Figure 80.

B - Start emery wheel. Slide cutter down post, flat edge
of blade against flat edge of stone. Then move cutter up
post. See Figure 81 below.

(Figure 81)

Cutter is sharpened by sliding cutter up
and down sharpening post.

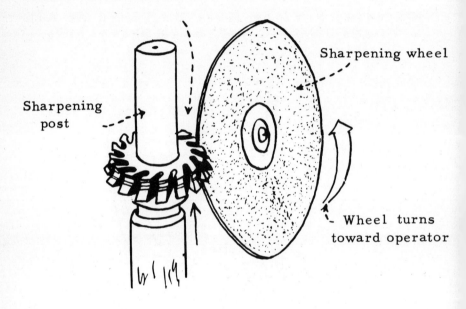

Sharpening
post

Sharpening wheel

Wheel turns
toward operator

C - Turn cutter to next blade and repeat above operation. Repeat the same on balance of blades.

D - Apply even light pressure on downward and upward
strokes.   Same amount of pressure must be applied to
each blade so that they are all sharpened evenly. Uneven
sharpening of blades will cause faulty trimming. Sharpen
cutter so that as they become worn with use and sharpening they will have the appearance of worn cutter as in Fig.
79.

2.   Operation of Trimmer.

A - Attach proper size of cutter for shoe to be trimmed.

B - Start trimmer which revolves at a high rate of speed and is motor driven.

C - Dampen edge of tap and welt with water. Water may be applied with either damp cloth, sponge or inking brush.

D - The trimming of the sole edge is done with three basic strokes. See Figure 82 below.

(Figure 82)

The starting and the ending points
of the three basic trimming strokes.

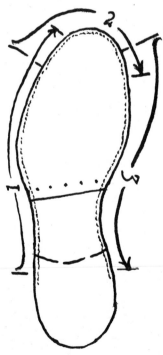

(Figure 83)

Position Of Hands For Holding Shoe
For First Trimming Stroke

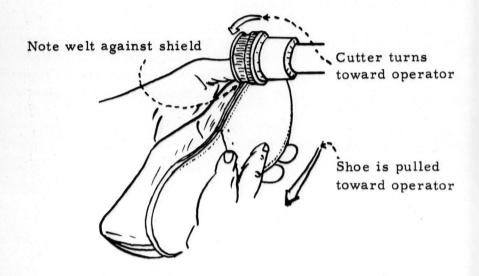

Note welt against shield

Cutter turns
toward operator

Shoe is pulled
toward operator

E - The first stroke.

(1) Grasp the shoe with the right hand holding the back of the counter or heel and with the under side of the shoe resting firmly between the thumb and fingers of the left hand. See Figure 83 above.

Thus the toe of the shoe is pointing away from the operator and the bottom of the shoe is perpendicular to the floor.   Hold the sole edge up to the under side of the cutter. See Fig. 82. Place the sole edge against the cutter so that the Guard Shield is between the shoe upper and the welt.   Hold the upper side of the welt against the guard shield throughout all trimming operations. The starting point for trimming should be at the heel breast. See Figure 82.

(2) Pull the shoe gently but firmly toward operator until the end of 1st stroke, as in Figure 82.   Be

sure that the same amount of pressure is applied entire distance of stroke.

(3) Remove shoe from cutter at end of stroke.

F - The Second Stroke.

(1) Move right hand so that it holds bottom of
shoe as in Figure 84.   Grasp upper of shoe with left
hand as in Figure 84 below.

(Figure 84)

Position Of Hands For Holding
Shoe For Second Trimming Stroke

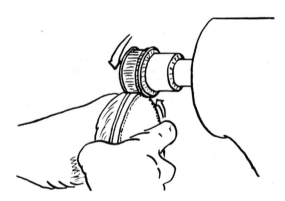

Shoe is pulled toward operator

(2) Place sole edge to cutter (toe pointing away
from operator) at a point on sole just back of where
lst stroke ended.

(3) Start pulling shoe toward operator and as
cutter approaches toe, swing shoe around so that cutter is going down opposite edge.   Swinging the shoe

around so that the toe is trimmed in one continuous even pressure motion is strictly a wrist movement. Toe must be trimmed without changing positions of the hands during the stroke. Considerable practice is necessary for this movement as even pressure must be applied throughout the stroke. Consult Figure 82 for starting and ending points of Stroke 2. At the end of second stroke, toe of shoe is pointing toward operator. Remove shoe from cutter.

G - The Third Stroke.

(1) Move the left hand so that it is grasping the upper of the shoe over the instep. Move the right hand so that the fingers are under the edge trimmed by 1st stroke. Place the right thumb against shoe bottom and parallel with the length of the sole. Toe of shoe is pointing toward operator.

(2) Apply the sole edge to the cutter at a point just back of where 2nd stroke ended. Consult Fig. 82.

(3) Pull the shoe with same amount of pressure as usual in first strokes. Trim edge to as near heel seat as possible. Consult Figure 82.

H - Even pressure applied to the cutter all the way around sole edge will result in a smooth, even edge.

I - To remove any raises or ridges in sole edge apply the shoe to the cutter again. Use same three strokes but use less pressure.

J - In trimming use the welt as a guide. Trim sole flush to welt. DO NOT trim off any of the welt.

K - To give the shoe an added "new shoe appearance" trim the edge of the outside of the shoe so that it flares out slightly. The edge around toe and on inside of

shoe should be trimmed straight up and down.   See
Figure 85 below.

(Figure 85)

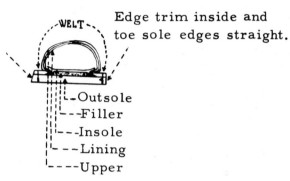

Edge trim outside
sole edge flared
out a trifle.

WELT

Edge trim inside and
toe sole edges straight.

—Outsole
---Filler
---Insole
---Lining
----Upper

L - Be sure that mates of the pair of shoes are trimmed
alike. Check by holding mates together. Both soles
should have the same shape and one should not protrude more than the other.

M - The sole edge is now ready to be burnished.

LESSON   12

SOLE   BURNISHING   MADE   EASY

The Burnisher Section of the Finisher consists of
two burnishing brushes, two burnishing wheels, bottom leveler and edge setter.

There are two each of the burnishing brushes and
wheels as one is used for black burnishing and the other
for brown. See Figure 86.

Burnishing Section

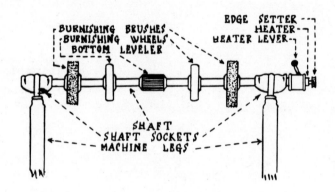

The Bottom Leveler is a ribbed, steel cylinder, used for closing the stitch channel. Some models of finishers are not equipped with bottom levelers but closing of channel without leveler will also be described.

The edge setter is a small ribbed, steel wheel the same size as the edge cutter. The edge setter is easily removed from the shaft.   When "setting" a sole edge the same size setter must be used to correspond with the size cutter used in edge trimming. See Figure 86 above.

1 - Inking Sole Edge.

A -   Grasp the upper of the shoe with left hand and hold shoe so that the bottom faces up and is horizontal to the floor.

B -   Take inking brush in right hand, dip it in color burnishing ink desired (Brown or Black). Holding the brush in a horizontal position start to apply ink on sole edge where trimming operation started.

C -   Draw the inking brush all the way around sole edge in one continous stroke. No pressure should be applied in this operation - hold brush lightly. Do not get any ink on shoe upper or on sole bottom.

D - Allow ink to dry.   This is important as it contains wax and enough time should be allowed so that the dye in the ink can penetrate the edge and the wax can "set" on the edge.

NOTE: Before using burnishing ink stir it thoroughly as the wax in the ink settles when it sets for any length of time.

E -   Start burnisher section in motion, which is motor driven.

F -   After ink has dried, grasp upper of shoe with left hand and the shank with the right hand. At the point where inking was started hold the edge up to front - center of burnishing brush. See Figure 87. Position of hands is not changed during this operation.   Turning of shoe on the burnishing brush is strictly a wrist movement.

2 - Bottom Leveling Sole

A -   Change the position of the shoe (from the above operation) so that the bottom faces up.   The left hand holds the shoe by the instep and right hand grasps the counter. See Figure 88.

B -   Close the stitch channel by holding shoe bottom up to bottom leveler. See Figure 88. Move shoe back and forth against bottom leveler until en - tire channel has been closed. Considerable pressure is needed in this operation.

Sole Burnishing

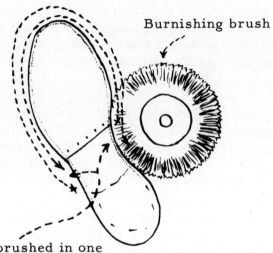

Burnishing brush

Sole edge is brushed in one
stroke from shank to shank.

Closing Stitch Channel
(Bottom Leveling)

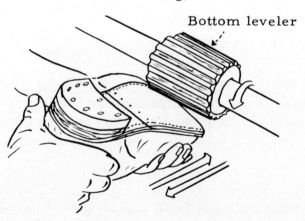

Bottom leveler

C - To close channel when no bottom leveler is available place the shoe on the last as in resoling . Grasp head of hammer in right hand and end of handle in left hand.   See Figure 89 below.   With pressure proceed to rub handle over entire channel thereby closing it.

Bottom Leveling By Hand

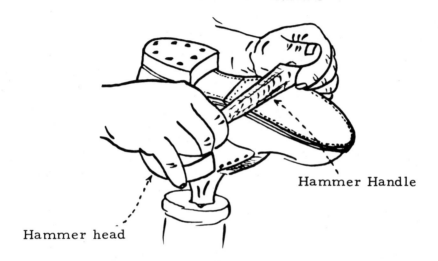

Hammer Handle

Hammer head

3 -   Edge   Setting

A -   Grasp shoe in same manner as in edge trimming.   See Figure 90.   Hold shoe up to edge setter in the same manner as in edge trimming. See Figure 90.

B - Start "setting" edge at the same point that trimming was started.

C - "Set" entire sole edge in one continuous movement.

(Figure 90)

Edge Setting

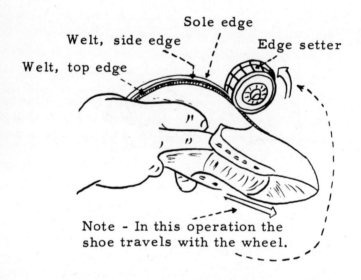

Welt, top edge

Welt, side edge

Sole edge

Edge setter

Note - In this operation the shoe travels with the wheel.

D - Unlike edge trimming, considerable pressure must be applied when edge setting.

E - On all makes of finishers a heating device is attached which warms the edge setter. Allow the setter to just get warm. The warmth of the heater plus friction heat of the sole edge against setter will cause the color to be baked on the sole edge. If setter is hot before edge setting starts, the leather may become burned resulting in uneven coloring of edge.

F - After setting, brush the sole edge lightly on the burnishing brush. It is important that entire edge be brushed in one movement. Circle sole edge several times lightly on burnishing brush and the result will be a bright, glossy edge.

4 -   Bottom Burnishing

A - Finishing of bottom is optional. Some operators leave the bottom with its natural color especially
when full soles have been put on shoes. Some operators
ink entire shoe bottom, heel to toe, with burnishing ink.
Other operators apply burnishing ink to only a portion
of bottom. There is available on the market bottom finishing paints which come in several colors and are used
mostly on the bottom of women's shoes.

B - To burnish entire bottom apply burnishing ink
to it. Allow ink to dry. After ink has dried hold shoe
bottom up to burnishing brush in the same manner as
bottom leveling.   Brush entire bottom.   Hold shoe
bottom up to burnishing wheel in same manner and
apply burnishing wax to entire bottom.   Next hold
bottom up to burnishing brush. Proceed to brush bottom with considerable pressure and in a circular motion. After entire bottom has been brushed with pressure, continue to brush bottom but gradually lessening
pressure. Continue to brush lightly in circular motion
until light, clear gloss is brought out.

C - To partially burnish bottom several designs
are used. With this type of finishing the main object
is to cover shank and sole joint. See Figure 91.

Apply burnishing ink on shank design. After ink
has dried, brush off. Apply burnishing wax as described above - then brush up to a gloss in same manner
as described above.

D - When using bottom finishing paints, stir paint
thoroughly and apply to entire shoe bottom with Camels'
Hair Paint Brush. Allow paint to dry. Rub lightly with
soft cloth. Bottom finish paints come in a varied
number of tan and cream colors.

(Figure 91)

Suggested Shank Designs

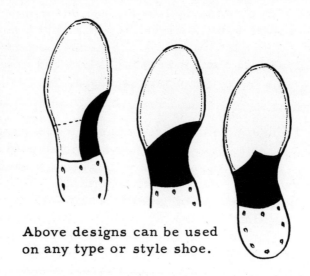

Above designs can be used
on any type or style shoe.

Above can also be used on full sole jobs.

LESSON   13

HOW MEN'S GOODYEAR WELT DOUBLE SOLED
SHOES   ARE   RESOLED

Double soled shoes are of two types. (1) A half
mid-sole (slip sole), is placed between the outer sole
and welt and extends from the toe back to the shank.
(2) Full mid-sole, extends from the toe over entire
shoe bottom to back of heel.

The mid-soles are placed on shoe bottom over filler. Outer sole is then placed over mid-sole, thus the

name "Double Soled Shoe." See Figure 92 below.

Two Types of Double Soled Shoes

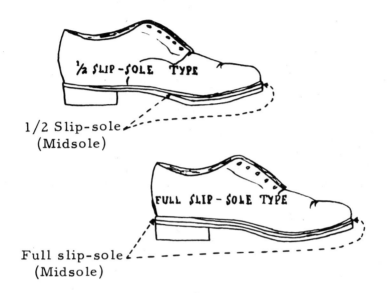

1/2 Slip-sole
(Midsole)

Full slip-sole
(Midsole)

1 - Resoling the Half Mid-Soled Shoe.

A - Measure tap at shank, draw line, cut off outer sole and skive shank the same as single sole procedure.

B - Take pincers in right hand and grasp the butt of the slip sole. "Peel" slip sole off with a rolling motion - shank to toe.

C - With straight knife cut off stitch threads left sticking up by removal of slip sole.

D - Check filler, inseam and welt same as in single sole procedure.

E - Remove stitches from welt.

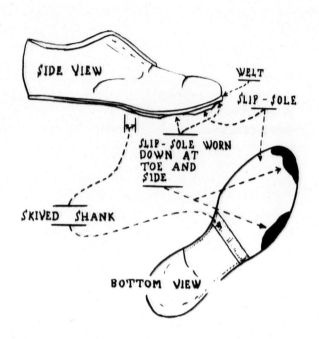

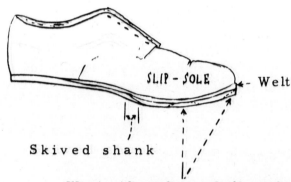

Worn side and toe of slip-sole
"squared - up" with skivings.
Refer to Figure 93.

F - Cement (with rubber cement) slip-sole back in place.

G - If slip sole is worn down on the toe or edges , "square up" worn places. See Fig. 93, page 92.

To "square up" worn parts sand off worn spots on sanding wheel, forming an even bevel. Cement skiving (pieces skived off butts of taps by skiving machine) on sanded worn spots. Trim skiving flush with welt. Sand top of skiving so that it is level with balance of shoe bottom. See Figure 94, page 92.

H - If slip sole is worn through in the center it is advisable to replace it. Trying to patch center of slip sole usually causes bumps and will be uncomfortable to wearer. When replacing slip soles be sure replacement is of the same thickness as the old one.

I - It is recommended that a piece of thin cloth be cemented on central part of slip sole. See Figure 95. This is done to prevent squeaking. Squeaks in shoes are usually caused by two pieces of leather rubbing together.

(Fig.   95)

"Squared-Up" Portions of Slip Sole

Attach piece of thin cloth to slip - sole to prevent squeaking.

Attach with rubber cement.

Skived shank.- - -

J - Apply rubber cement over entire surface to be resoled. Allow to dry.

K - Now that the shoe is prepared, proceed to resole by the same procedure as in single sole operations. Nailing tap at shank, stitching, trimming, edge setting and brushing are the same as soling single soled shoe.

2 - Resoling Full Mid-Soled Shoe.

A - Cut off outer sole and skive shank the same as in single sole procedure.

B - "Peel" mid-sole back from toe to shank. Cut off stitches, remove stitches from welt, check filler, inseam and welt same as in single-sole procedure. Cement mid-sole back in place.

C - If mid-sole is worn down on edges, "square up" the same as in the slip-sole operation.

D - If mid-sole is worn through in the center cut off mid-sole at the shank just above where the outsole skive ends. Skive mid-sole and fit in new mid-sole. Remember to cement replacement in position.

E - Proceed to resole the same as in single sole operations.

LESSON 14

THE STANDARD METHOD OF RESOLING MEN'S GOODYEAR WELT SHOE WITH FULL SOLE

Resoling shoes with full soles has become very popular for it gives the repaired shoe more of a "like new" appearance. Many customers have this done as they feel it gives them new support in the shank.

1 -   Single Soled   Shoe

A -   Remove entire heel from shoe.

B - About an inch back from heel breast line draw a line across the heel seat. See Figure 96.

C - Rip off entire sole from heel breast forward.

D -   Butt sole at heel breast.

E -   From line draw across heel seat skive forward.   Skive should be about 3/4 inch wide and down to a feather edge. See Figure 96 below.

Heel Seat Skived Preparatory To Full Soling

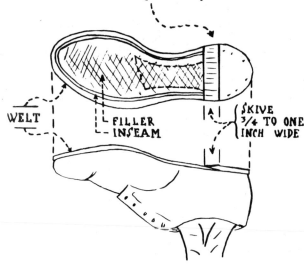

F -   Check inseam, welt and filler the same as in single 1/2 sole operation.

G - Check shank piece. If shank piece is broken, replace it. See Figure 97.

NOTE: - All shoes have pieces in the shank to aid the support of the arch.   Shank pieces may be of wood or steel. Shank pieces are available from jobbers.

(Figure 97)

Shank Piece Is Inserted In Shoe To Aid
In Holding Its Shape And Give Support
To The Wearer's Arch

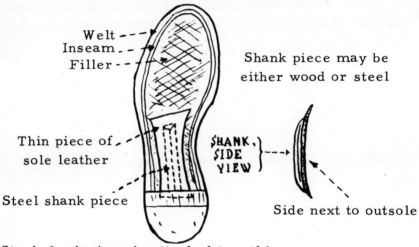

Welt
Inseam
Filler

Shank piece may be
either wood or steel

Thin piece of
sole leather

SHANK,
SIDE
VIEW

Steel shank piece

Side next to outsole

Steel shank piece is attached to a thin
piece of sole leather to prevent its
breaking thru the insole.

H -   Skive butt of full sole the same as butt of tap.

I - Mold full sole same as tap.

J -   Place butt of full sole in position on heel seat skive. Secure with two nails.

K - Lay full sole forward, shaping sole over shank and then laying sole down over ball part of shoe and to toe .

L - Tap sole lightly over entire surface to insure fusing of rubber cement on full sole and bottom of shoe.

M - Trim sole edge with lip knife as in single half soling procedure.

N - When stitching sole start stitching at beginning of welting just back of heel breast.   Continue stitching around to end of welting on opposite side.

O - Proceed to edge trim and burnish sole edge as in 1/2 sole operation.

P - Reheel, insert heel pad and skive shoes. Shoe is ready for the customer. Reheeling will be described in a separate chapter.

2   -   Full-Soling Double Soled Shoe.

A - Double soled shoe is resoled with full sole by the same method as outlined above.

Checking of mid-sole is the same as for 1/2 sole operation.

LESSON   15

HOW TO PUT AN INVISIBLE HALF-SOLE ON MEN'S GOODYEAR WELT SHOE

Invisible 1/2 soling is attaching the sole of the shoe with a waterproof celluloid Leather Cement instead of by other methods.   There are two types of invisible 1/2 soling: (1) Attaching sole at the shank with leather cement, instead of nailing, and then stitching sole as usual; (2) attaching entire sole with leather cement.

(Figure 98)

One Model Of Cement Press

Hydraulic Cement Press

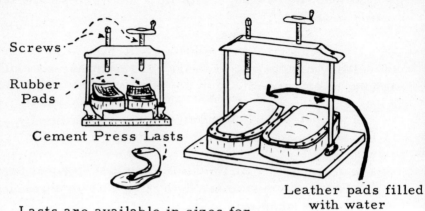

Screws

Rubber
Pads

Cement Press Lasts

Leather pads filled
with water

Lasts are available in sizes for
men's, women's, and children's shoes.

(Figure 99)

One Model Of The Shank Press

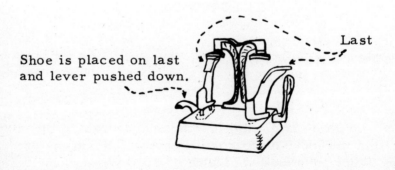

Last

Shoe is placed on last
and lever pushed down.

To do the attaching of the sole, the leather cement is applied to both the shoe bottom and tap and then the shoe is placed in especially designed shoe press. See Fig. 98. If sole is to be attached by cementing the shank only the shoe can be pressed in either a shoe press or in a especially designed shank press. See Fig. 99.

There are several makes of shoe presses on the market with each having special features but the principle of all is the same.

The basic principle of the shoe press is fitting a proper size last in the shoe, placing the shoe on a cushion pad and then pressing the shoe down on the pad with as much pressure as possible.

The different makes of presses vary as to the type of cushion pad and method of applying the pressure.

The pads in presses vary from sponge rubber to leather pads inflated with air and some with water.

Some make presses are equipped with electric heating elements to speed the drying of the cement; these are known as Hot Presses. Those without the heating element are known as Cold Presses.

The choice of a type of press is merely a matter of personal opinion. All presses on the market are designed to do the same job and are all tested and proved before being placed on the market.

Invisible half soling is the modern method of attaching soles and should be used whenever humanly possible. Invisible soling is recommended because it gives the repaired shoe a "like-new" appearance. Along with that it will allow a pair of shoes to be resoled oftener and it gives more comfort to the wearer.

Invisible half soling is your best salesman and advertisement.

Invisible soling can be used on all shoes to be repaired with Oak Leather. It cannot be used with rubber taps.

Regular Oak Sole Leather is commonly known as Hard Oak.   For invisible soling purposes all tanneries process what is known as Flexible Oak Leather.   However, both types are used for invisible soling.

Flexible Oak sole leather is just what the name implies for it is very pliable and does not need to be tempered to be used.

Flexible leather comes in the same cuts and grades as Hard Oak. It also comes in weights adaptable for both men's and women's shoes.

Although Flexible leather comes in all grades, and all grades can be used for the cement method, for the best results use only the better grade if possible.

1 - Invisible, or cement, method for Men's Goodyear Welt Single-Sole Shoe - Hard Oak Leather.

A - Preparation of taps.

(1) Skive butt of tap, same as in previous operations.

(2) Rough skive with a special Roughing Tool or Brush by hand or by Special Roughing Wheel attached to finisher. See Figures 100 and 101. Roughing tools are designed for this purpose, by all means use them.

(3) Rough balance of flesh side of tap with rasp or on finisher sanding wheel as in previous operations.

(Figure   100)

Roughing Tools

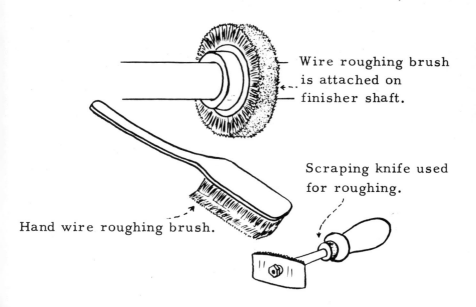

Wire roughing brush
is attached on
finisher shaft.

Scraping knife used
for roughing.

Hand wire roughing brush.

(Figure   101)

Skived Tap Butt Roughed
Prior To Applying Leather Cement

(4) On the flesh side of tap brush off all loose particles with stiff bristle brush.

(5) Apply thin coat of Leather cement on roughed skive. Brush leather cement in evenly and work into leather thoroughly. See Figure 102.

(6) Apply rubber cement to balance of tap as usual. See Figure 102.

(7) After both cements have dried thoroughly proceed to temper taps as usual.

(8) In order to speed up production it is recommended that several pairs of taps always be prepared and tempered in advance.

(Figure   102   )

Apply Rubber Cement To
Surface Beyond Skive

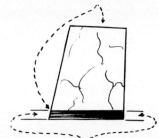

Apply leather cement to roughed skive.

B - Preparation of Shoe.

(1) Remove heel as in previous operations.

(2) Remove old sole and skive shank to a feather edge in the usual manner.

(3) Check welt, inseam, filler and remove old stitches from welt in usual manner.

(4) Rough skive with roughing tool, same as butt of tap. See Figure 103.

(5) Rough welt with rasp or on sanding wheel. See Figure 103.

(6) Clean Bottom of shoe thoroughly with stiff bristle brush.

(7) Apply thin coat of leather cement to skive, brush in thoroughly. See Figure 103.

(8) Apply thin coat of rubber cement to balance of shoe bottom. See Figure 103.

(9) Allow both cements to dry thoroughly. Drying time for leather cement is from 4 to 8 minutes, depending on atmosphere and room temperature.

(Figure 103)

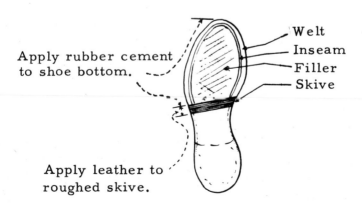

Apply rubber cement to shoe bottom.

Welt
Inseam
Filler
Skive

Apply leather to roughed skive.

C - Attaching the Sole.

(1) Apply a second thin coat of leather cement to the skived shank of the shoe.

(2) Place the tap on the shoe in its proper place. Pound the sole with hammer over area that rubber cement has been applied.

(3) Remove shoe from jack and fit press last into shoe. Be Sure the last fits the shoe properly.

(4) Place shoe in cement press. Be sure even pressure is applied to the shoe. See Figure 104.

(5) Leave shoe in press until cement has dried. Drying time in press will range from 20 to 30 minutes depending on type of press and room temperature.

NOTE: Due to the speed with which leather cement dries, the above operations must be done as quickly as possible. Work on one shoe at a time when attaching sole. The quicker the shoe is put in the press the better.

(6) After shoe has dried, remove it from press. If time permits it is advisable to leave shoe set out of press for a few minutes before trimming.

(7) Trim off excess leather from edges, with lip knife, as in previous operations for welt shoe.

(8) Take shoe to bottom sanding wheel on finisher and proceed to sand (scour) bottom of shoe in the following manner:
a- Grasp upper of the shoe, over the instep, with left hand, right hand holding the counter. Hold shoe with bottom facing up and toe pointing away from operator. See Figure 105.
b- Apply bottom of shoe to u n d e r   s i d e of

(Figure 104)

Shoe Placed In Cement Press

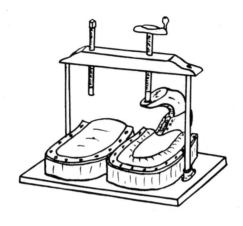

(Figure 105)

Sanding Shoe Bottom
(Scouring)

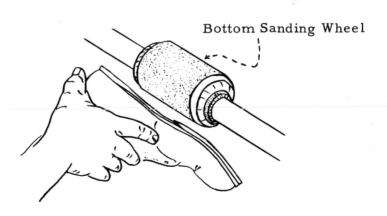

Bottom Sanding Wheel

sanding wheel just back of heel breast line. See Figures 105 and 106.

(Figure 106)

Arrows indicate path of scouring.

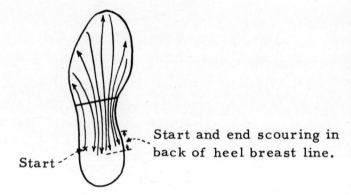

Start

Start and end scouring in back of heel breast line.

      c- Pull shoe (on sanding wheel) toward toe in straight line. Then push back - repeat these operations until entire surface of bottom has been sanded and shank joint is perfectly level with bottom shank. See Figures 106 and 107.

      d- Scour shank of shoe until all old stain is removed. In other words, the entire bottom should have the appearance of a full sole job. Only a faint line should be visible at the joint of the shank and tap butt.

      e- Bottom must be scoured with fast strokes and with very little pressure. The bottom of the tap should be scoured just enough to remove the grain and give tap a velvety appearance. A slow stroke or heavy pressure of tap against sanding wheel will result in burning tap and giving it an uneven color. Added pressure may be necessary at the shank in order to remove old stains and level tap butt.

      (9) Shoe is now ready to be stitched. Start stitching at the beginning of welt under heel seat. End

(Figure 107)

Bottom before scouring.
Note tap ridge at shank.

Bottom after scouring. Note smooth shank
line giving shoe "like - new" appearance.

stitching on opposite side at the end of welt. This operation will aid in giving the bottom a full-sole appearance -
hence, the Invisible Half Sole.   It cannot be seen that it
has been half soled.

(10) Edge trim, level bottom, and edge set
the same as in previous soling operation.

(11) Bottom may be burnished but if a careful scouring job has been done, bottom will need no further finishing.

(12) Attach heel, finish and insert heel pad.
Shine the uppers and shoe will look as near like new as

is possible to do.

> 2 - Invisible Method for Men's Goodyear
> Welt Single -Soled Shoe - Flexible Oak.

A - Preparation of Tap.

(1) As tap is flexible it needs no tempering .

(2) Skive butt, rough skive with roughing tool.

(3) Rough balance of tap with rasp or sand - ing wheel.

(4) Brush off all loose particles with stiff bristle brush.

(5) Apply thin coat of leather cement on roughed skive add thin coat of rubber cement on balance of tap. Work cements in thoroughly.

(6) Allow cements to dry.

(7) Tap is now ready for attaching.

B - Preparation of Shoe.

(1) Shoe is prepared exactly the same as for attaching Hard Oak tap by cement method.

C - Attaching Tap.

(1) Tap is attached and shoe is placed in shoe press the same as with Hard Oak tap. Trim, scour bottom, stitch, edge trim, level bottom, and edge set as in cement method for Hard Oak tap.

(2) Although flexible tap does not need to be tempered it is advisable to welt bottom of tap before stitching.   This is recommended to eliminate possibility of grain side of tap cracking.

3 - Invisible Resoling Double-Soled Goodyear Welt Men's Shoe.

A - Preparation of Tap.

(1) Tap is prepared exactly the same as for Single-sole cement method.

B - Preparation of Shoe.

(1) Same procedure is followed as when preparing double-soled shoe for nailing shank.

(2) Shank is prepared the same as shank of single-soled shoe cement method.

C - Attaching Tap.

(1) Tap is attached the same as described in previous cement method.

(2) Trim, scour bottom, stitch, edge trim, level bottom, and edge set the same as in previous invisible operations.

4 -   Invisible Resoling Men's Goodyear Welt Single-Soled Shoe With Cement Only.

A - Preparation of Shoe.

(1) Remove old sole as in previous operations.

(2) Skive shank in usual manner. Pull up skived shank for 1/2 to 1 inch behind where it is cut off. See Figure 108.

(3) Rough under part of shank with special shank rasp. This rasp is thin, and coarse on both sides so it will rough up both under part of shank and welt at the same time. See Figure 108.

(Figure 108)

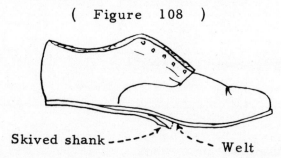

Skived shank - - - - - - -   Welt

Skived shank is "peeled" back a trifle beyond skive. Under side of shank and welt are roughed and leather cement applied to roughed surfaces.

(4) Clean all foreign matter from top of shoulder (rib of insole), inseam and welt on sanding wheel.

(5) Rough with roughing tool, skive, welt and inseam.

(6) Apply thin coat of leather cement to skive, welt and inseam, brushing in cement thoroughly. See Figure 109.

(7) Apply rubber cement to filler. See Figure 109.

(8) Allow both cements to dry.

B - Preparation of tap.

NOTE: Flexible or Hard Oak tap can be used for this job but Flexible Oak is preferable.   Both types of tap are prepared the same except that the Hard Oak tap is tempered after cements have been applied.

(Figure 109)

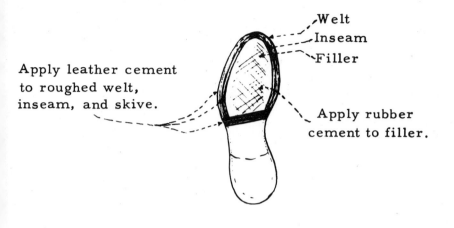

Apply leather cement
to roughed welt,
inseam, and skive.

Welt

Inseam

Filler

Apply rubber
cement to filler.

(Figure 110)

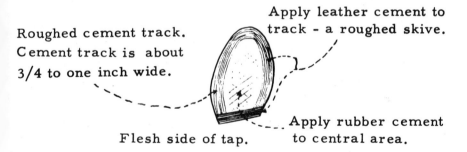

Apply leather cement to
track - a roughed skive.

Roughed cement track.
Cement track is about
3/4 to one inch wide.

Flesh side of tap.

Apply rubber cement
to central area.

(1) Using old sole as a pattern, cut new tap
so that it is about 1/8 inch larger all around than the old
sole.

(2) Skive butt as usual.

(3) Using roughing tool rough shank and about
one inch in width all the way around edge of tap.   (See
Figure 110) .

(4) Clean flesh side of tap thoroughly with stiff bristle brush.

(5) Apply thin coat of leather cement on roughed shank and edge, brush in thoroughly. (See Figure 110).

(6) Apply rubber cement in the center of tap. (See Figure 110).

(7) Allow both cements to dry.

C - Attaching Tap.

(1) Select press last to be used - last must be proper size and shape to fit shoe properly.

(2) Apply a second thin coat of leather cement to the roughed parts of the shoe.

(3) Place prepared tap in proper position on shoe. Fasten it in place with two lasting tacks at the shank. Do not drive tacks clear in - - leave them protrude just enough so that they can be removed later.

(4) Place press last in shoe and place shoe in position while pressure is being applied to shoe.

(5) Remember, speed is very necessary in the above operations so that the cement does not dry before the shoe is in the press. Work on one shoe at a time in this operation.

(6) After shoes have dried in the press (20 to 30 minutes) remove and allow them to set for a few minutes.

(7) Trim sole edge with lip knife.

(8) Edge trim, scour bottom and edge set as usual. Sole is not stitched as it is fastened with leather cement.

5 - Invisible Resoling Double-Soled Goodyear Welt Shoe With Cement Only.

A - Preparation of Shoe.

(1) Remove old sole and skive shank as usual.

(2) Remove slip sole and cut off protruding stitches and remove stitches as usual.

(3) Check welt, inseam, and filler as usual.

(4) Cement slip sole back in position and check worn spots on same.

(5) Stitch slip sole to welt on stitching ma - chine. Start and end stitching back of skive.

(6) With roughing tool rough skive and 3/4 to 1 inch strip all around edge of slip sole. (Figure 111).

(7) Brush off all loose particles as usual.

(8) Apply thin coat of leather cement on roughed parts. Work cement in thoroughly. (See Figure 111) .

(9) Cement, with rubber cement, piece of thin cloth on center of slip sole. (See Figure 111) .

(10) Allow cement to dry thoroughly.

B - Preparation of Tap.

Tap is prepared in the same manner as cemen- ting single-soled shoe. (Paragraph 4-B above) .

(Figure 111)

Rough cement track
3/4 inch wide.

Attach piece of thin
cloth to central area.

Apply leather cement
to cement track.

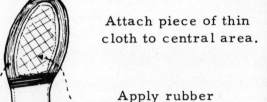

Apply rubber
cement to cloth.

C - Attaching Tap.

  The same operations are used as for attaching
and pressing tap in single-soled shoe. (Paragraph 4-C,
above) .

D - Finishing.

  Edge trim, scour bottom and edge-set to finish
as usual.

LESSON   16

HOW   MEN'S   NAILED   SHOES   ARE   RESOLED.

Men's nailed shoes are of two types of construction
(1) A single out sole nailed to insole. (See Figure 112)
(2) A mid-sole and out sole are attached to give shoe
goodyear welt appearance. This is done by stitching outsole and midsole with goodyear welt stitches; then nailing
the two soles to the insole. When resoling this type shoe,

and to give it a like-new appearance, employ the same
method as used in making the shoe.

(Figure   112)

Nailed Shoe -
Double Soled Type

Nailed Shoe -
Single Soled Type

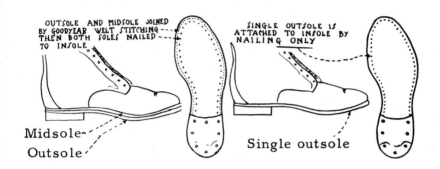

Midsole

Outsole

Single outsole

1 - Resoling Midsole Type.

A - Preparation of Shoe.

(1) Measure new tap on the shoe the same
as when 1/2 soling welt type shoe.

(2) Insert corner of straight knife between
outsole and midsole and proceed to cut stitches all the
way around sole from shank line to shank line.

(3) With the pincers grasp the outsole at
the toe.   Using a rolling motion "peel" the outsole
loose from the nails back to the shank.   (See Figure
113) .

(4) About an inch ahead of shank line-cut off
worn sole the same as in welt sole operations.   Skive
shank as usual.

(Figure 113)

''Peeling'' Worn Sole Off Nailed Type Shoe

Note: Sole removal starts at toe.

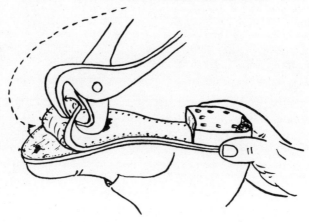

(5) With pincers remove all old nails that may remain in midsole as far back as skive of shank.

(6) Check worn spots of midsole the same as in welt double-soled operations.

(7) Check upper to see if it is tacked to insole all the way around. Wherever upper is loose tack it in place with lasting tacks.

(8) Apply thin coat of rubber cement to bottom of insole and bottom side of midsole. Allow cement to dry.

(9) Lay midsole back in place and pound with hammer over entire surface.

(10) Rough top side of midsole with rasp or on sanding wheel.

(11) Apply thin coat of rubber cement to top midsole surface. Allow to dry.

B - Preparation of Tap.

(1) Prepare hard oak tap as in Chapter 6 "Preparation of Soles ".

C - Attaching Tap.

(1) Place tap in position and nail butt of tap the same as soling welt type shoe. It is suggested that when resoling work (heavy) shoes a double row of nails be placed across the shank to insure better holding. (See Figure 47 .)

(2) Lay tap down on midsole, pound tap over entire surface to insure good joint between outsole and midsole.

(3) Place one nail up near the toe of the sole about 3/4 inch in from the toe edge. Use a long enough nail so that it will just touch the last and will stick above the tap surface enough so that it can be removed later.

(4) Remove shoe from last. With lip knife trim outsole flush with midsole edge.

(5) With pincer press midsole and outsole edges together to insure better joint between the two.

(6) Stitch insole and outsole together on good-year welt stitching machine the same as stitching welt shoe.

(7) Place shoe back on last. Drive nails all around the edge of tap as shown in Figure 114. Place the nails in a neat even line. The line of nails should be the same distance in from the sole edge as the original nail line. (See Figure 114). Space the nails about 3/8 to 1/2

inch apart - - keep them as evenly spaced as possible,
(see Figure 114) . Remember, neatness in workmanship is an operator's biggest asset.

(Figure   114)

Resoled Nailed-Shoe
Double - Soled Type

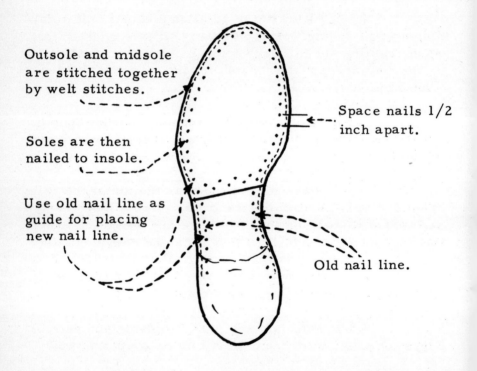

Outsole and midsole
are stitched together
by welt stitches.

Space nails 1/2
inch apart.

Soles are then
nailed to insole.

Use old nail line as
guide for placing
new nail line.

Old nail line.

(8) Pull out nail placed near the toe edge.

(9) Remove shoe from last, feel inside for
nails that may not have clinched.

(10) Proceed to edge trim and edge set as
in previous operations.

2 - Resoling Single-Sole Nailed Shoe (No Mid-Sole)

A - Preparation of Shoe.

(1) Measure tap on shoe and draw shank line as usual.

(2) With pincers grasp toe of worn sole and "peel" it back to shank line.

(3) "Butt" old sole as usual.

(4) Remove all nails remaining in shoe bottom.

(5) Skive shank as usual.

(6) Check upper lasted to insole. Tack loose upper in place with lasting tacks.

(7) Rough bottom of shoe with rasp or on sanding wheel.

(8) Apply thin coat of rubber cement on shoe bottom. Allow cement to dry.

B - Preparation of Tap.

(1) Prepare Hard Oak tap as in Chapter 6 "Preparation of Soles."

C - Attaching Tap.

(1) Place tap in position and nail shank as in previous operations.

(2) Lay tap down on shoe bottom. Pound tap over entire surface to insure joint between tap and shoe bottom.

(3) Remove shoe from last. With lip knife trim edges following the shape of innersole as a guide. When trimming this type shoe trim tap so that it is about 1/16 to 1/8 inch wider (all the way around) than original sole. This is done because when tap is nailed it will "pull up" about that amount in shaping.

(4) Proceed to nail tap as in previous method for nailed type shoe.

(5) Edge trim and edge set as usual.

NOTE: Of late years Stapling and other types of wire fastening machines have been perfected that take the place of hand nailing. Wherever nails are used stapling machines can be used.

Due to the fact that the operation of different makes of wire fastening machines vary they cannot be described here. Complete directions for this operation are furnished by the manufacturer.

The principle of all makes of stapling machines is the same. Wire is fed thru the machine and is cut off at the desired length to correspond to nail length. As the pieces of wire are cut off they are automatically driven in the shoe - in other words, automatic nailing.

It goes without saying that with a wire fastening machine a tap can be attached to a shoe in considerably less time than by hand nailing.

Figure 115 illustrates one type of stapler

(Figure 115)

Electric Auto Soler

LESSON XVII

HOW TO RESOLE LADIES' SHOES

The operations used for repairing ladies' shoes in most cases are the same as applied to the resoling of men's shoes. The biggest difference is in the weight (thickness) of materials used.

Ladies' taps will vary from 4 to 5 iron, for dress shoes, to 8 or 8 1/2 for work shoes.

As a rule, women want thin soles, yet expect the same wearing quality of thicker soles. To do this skive around the entire edge of tap (flesh side) to thickness desired. When sole is finished, the thin edges will give the appearances of thin soled shoes yet will be thicker where it is given the most wear.

Hard or flexible leathers may be used. Hard Oak taps should be tempered as described in Chapter 6 - "Preparation of Soles." It is recommended that whenever possible flexible leather should be used on ladies' shoes. As a rule, women demand and need more flexibility in their shoes than men. Also, due to the fact that as a rule women's shoes are considerably smaller than men's shoes, the new tap requires more shaping.

Remember, always, that women do the majority of the shopping. Cater to them by doing neat workmanship, and by keeping yourself and shop neat at all times. Practically every woman admires and demands neatness where she spends her money.

Ladies shoes for the most part are constructed by one of three methods:

(1) Goodyear Welt - - usually oxfords with cuban or low heels and are designed for dress, work, nurses, and spectator sport styles.

(2) McKay - - This type is used in making ladies shoes for practically every use.

(3) Cement - - Most commonly adopted for dress shoes.

1 -   Resoling Ladies Goodyear Welt Shoes:

A - All types of ladies Goodyear Welt shoes are resoled by exactly the same operations as used on Men's Goodyear Welt Shoes.

Shanks may be nailed or cemented but it is strongly recommended that cemented shanks used on all ladies shoes if humanly possible.

2 - Resoling Cement Type Ladies Shoes.

A -   Preparation of Shoes.

(1) Measure tap, mark shank as usual.

(2) With the pincers rip old sole from the shoe starting at the toe and working back. This must be done very carefully as the materials of the uppers are usually very thin. If the old sole is pulled off fast, the upper may be torn.   If it appears that the old sole will be difficult to remove, without tearing upper, apply a small amount of leather cement THINNER along   the edge with a brush.   ·Be sure to hold the shoe toe down so that the thinner will not run under the shank.   The sole now should come off with ease.

(3) Skive shank to feather edge as usual.

(4) Rough skive with roughing tool. On factory cement type shoes the bottom has been roughed so it will not be necessary to rough it unless old sole has been worn down to upper. In that case, rough only worn part, being very careful not to tear upper.

(5) If upper has come unlasted at any place, (upper loose from insole) relast in the following man- ner:

(a) Remove filler.

(b) Rough insole and underside of upper.

(c) Apply thin coat of leather ce- ment to roughed parts. Allow cement to dry.

(d) Apply second coat of leather cement to roughed parts.   Pull upper into place and secure temporarily with lasting tacks.

(e) After leather cement is dry, re-move lasting tacks. Replace filler, cement it in place with rubber cement.

(6) Remove any leather particles that may be in old cement track on shoe. It is not necessary to remove the old leather cement as the new cement will soften it and form with it.

(7) Apply thin coat of leather cement to roughed parts and rubber cement to filler. See Figure 116. Allow cements to dry.

(Figure   116)

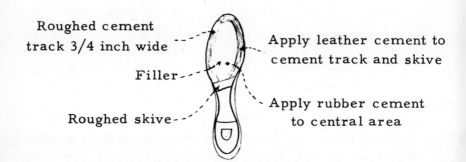

Roughed cement
track 3/4 inch wide

Filler

Roughed skive

Apply leather cement to
cement track and skive

Apply rubber cement
to central area

B - Preparation of Tap.

Tap is prepared the same as in previous cementing operations. Rough 3/4 inch cement track around tap edge. Apply leather cement to cement track and rubber cement to center. See Figure 117.

(Figure 117)

Ladies' Tap

Roughed cement track
3/4 inch wide

Apply leather cement to
cement track and skive

Flesh side of tap

Apply rubber cement
to central area

Roughed skive

C - Attaching Tap.

(1) Tap is attached and pressed the same
as described in Chapter 15, Paragraph 4c.

(2) Trim sole edge with lip knife. Follow the
shape of the innersole as a guide. Allow outsole to protrude about 1/16 of an inch beyond innersole. See Figure
118.

(3) Edge trim, scour bottom and edge set as
usual.

Many operators apply bottom finish to ladies shoe
bottoms. It is highly recommended for use on womens
shoes for appearance sake which in turn results in more
resoles.

NOTE: Cement type shoes may be resoled by nailing,
stapling, or by stitching on McKay stitcher. Follow same
operation as described in Paragraph 2 - "Resoling McKay
Type".

(Figure 118)

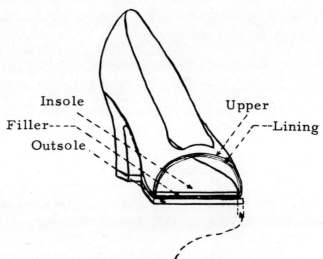

Using insole as a guide, trim outsole to
protrude 1/16 to 1/8 of an inch beyond insole.

3. Resoling McKay Type Shoes.

This type shoe can be resoled by stitching, cementing, stapling, or nailing.   Unless it cannot be avoided ,
the nailing method is not recommended for nailing the tap
on makes the shoe stiff and the job is not as neat appearing.

For those shoe repairmen that do not have a McKay
Stitcher or Stapler, it is recommended that the cement

method be used on all McKay type shoes if possible.

A - Resoling McKay Type By Cement Method.

   (1) Preparation of shoe.

      (a) Remove old sole by cutting old
stitches the same as in preparing welt types. Do not pull
old sole off with pincers.

      (b) Cut old sole off at shank as usual.

      (c) Skive shank to feather edge as usual.

      (d) Relast upper wherever loose the
same as described in Paragraph 2-A-(5) this chapter.

      (e) Check filler as usual.

      (f) With roughing tool, rough skive
and make cement track around edge of shoe bottom. See
Figure 116.

      (g) With stiff bristle brush remove all
loose and foreign particles from shoe bottom.

      (h) Apply thin coat of leather cement
to skive and cement track on shoe bottom. Brush cement
in thoroughly and allow to dry.   Apply rubber cement to
filler and allow to dry. See Figure 116.

   (2) Preparation of Tap.

   Tap is prepared the same as in previous cementing
operations.   Refer to Paragraph 2-B and Figure 117,
this chapter.

   (3) Attaching Tap.

Tap is attached and pressed the same as described in

Chapter 15, Paragraph 4-C. Finish shoe as described in this Chapter, Paragraph 2-C.

B - Resoling McKay Type Shoes by Stitching.

Taps may be attached at the shank by either nailing, stapling or cementing. The cement method is recommended if it is humanly possible to do so.   Whichever plan is used, prepare the tap by the same method as used for attaching sole to Goodyear Welt type shoe.   Refer to Chapter 7.

Cement type shoes may be resoled by the method described in this Paragraph.

(1)   Preparation of Shoe.

(a)   Remove sock liner from inside shoe.

(b)   Remove old sole by cutting stitches as described in Paragraph 3-A.

(c)   Cut off old sole and skive as usual. If shank is to be cemented, rough and apply thin coat of leather cement the same as resoling Welt type shoe.

(d)   Relast upper wherever loose.

(e)   Check filler.

(f)   Remove any lasting tacks or wire brads that may be in stitch line.

(g)   Apply thin coat of rubber cement to bottom (Shank to toe).   Allow cement to dry.

(h)   If innersole is curled or hard, dampen with water, place shoe on last and pound.   This may be done to innersole of any type shoe.

(2) Preparation of Tap.

Taps are prepared the same as for stitching tap on Goodyear Welt Type shoe. If shank is to be nailed merely skive butt of tap, rough and apply rubber cement to entire flesh side surface.

(Figure 119)

Rounding & Channeling Machine

This machine will trim sole edge, replacing hand trimming, and channels the sole in the same operation. The machine can also be used for trimming all sole edges regardless of the type of fastening that is used and the channel attachment can be thrown out of gear.

(3) Attaching Tap.

(a) Place tap in position on shoe. Attach butt to shank by either cementing, stapling or nailing.

(b) Lay tap down on shoe bottom and pound entire surface to insure joining of tap to shoe bottom.

(c) Remove shoe from last and prepare to trim by hand.   Following the shape of the inner sole, trim the outsole so that it protrudes about an 1/8 of an inch all the way around the shoe. See Figure 118.

(d) Scour shank and tap bottom as usual.

(e) Sole is now ready to be channeled and grooved.   There are several types of channelers and groovers. Figure 119 illustrates one model of channeler. The operation of the different makes of channelers vary but the results obtained from each is the same.

(f) The sole should be dry when channeling is done.   Adjust channeler so that the <u>outside</u> edge of the channel is in from the sole edge about <u>1/16</u> of an inch. See Figure 120. The <u>inside</u> of the channel should be in far enough so that it is just past the old stitch line.   Moisten with water and lay back the channel flap. See Figure 121. At the bottom of the channel cut the groove which should be in a line with the old stitch line in the shoe. See Figure 121.

(g) When stitching ladies shoes on McKay Stitcher use 4 strand stitching thread and adjust machine so that it makes about 4 1/2 stitches to the inch.

(h) Shoe is now ready to be stitched on McKay Stitcher. Figure 122 illustrates one model of McKay Stitcher.

(Figure 120)

Adjust Channeler So That Outside Edge Of Channel
Is About 1/16 Of An Inch In From Sole Edge

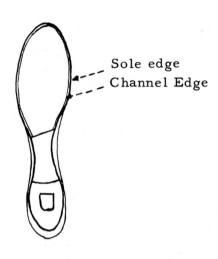

Sole edge
Channel Edge

(Figure 121)

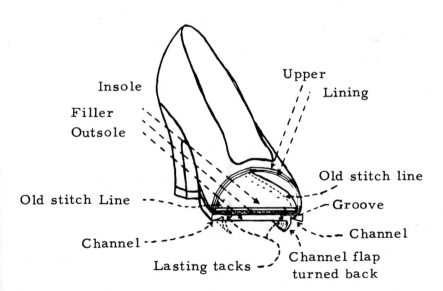

Insole

Filler
Outsole

Upper
Lining

Old stitch line

Old stitch Line

Groove

Channel

Channel

Lasting tacks

Channel flap
turned back

(Figure   122   )

Repco Sole Sewing Machine -   Model A

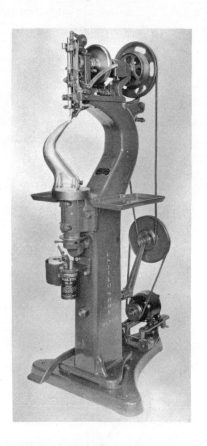

(i) Set Horn of stitcher so that it is
to the left of the machine and parallel with the front of
the machine. See Figure 123.

(j) Place shoe on Horn so that the
Horn is on the inside of the shoe facing up and the toe
of the shoe is pointing toward the right of the operator.
See Figure 123. Shoe should set so that shank joint is
in line with the needle.

(k) Set feed (the part that "feeds"
the shoe while being stitched) so that it is squarely in

in the base of the channel. - This is very important.

(Figure 123)

Position of shoe prior to
operation of Mc Kay stitcher.

Note position of
hands and horn

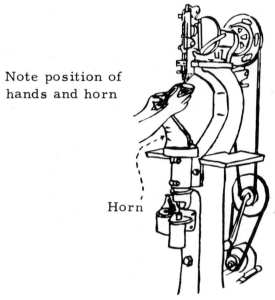

Horn

(l) Hold shoe at a slight angle so
that the bottom of shoe tips down toward machine - this
aids in helping to stay on innersole while stitching.

(m) Be sure presser foot holds shoe
down firmly.

(n) To start machine give fly wheel
a couple of turns with right hand then press foot pedal
to operate. Speed of machine is regulated by adding or
lessening pressure on foot pedal.

(o) Stitching around the toe is a little
difficult, especially on a narrow-toed shoe but can easily
be mastered with practice. When stitching McKay type

shoes one continuous stitch line should be your goal
the same as when Goodyear welt stitching.

(p) After stitching completely
around tap cut thread behind needle. Remove shoe
from horn.

(q) Apply rubber cement to bot-
tom side of channel flap. Allow cement to dry, then
close channel by rubbing flap down evenly.

(r) Edge trim, edge set, and finish
bottom as usual.

C - Resoling McKay Type With Stapler.

By this method prepare shoe and tap the same as
described above. Instead of stitching, staple in the
channel. Finish shoe as usual.

LESSON   18

HOW TO REPAIR TOE TIPS

As a rule when wearing high heeled shoes women
wear out the heels and the tips of the toes on their
shoes. Featuring the repair of toe tips means addi-
tional and profitable business for the operator.

Most women are "economy minded" so if they
can get the toe tips of their shoes replaced, without
having to get an entire sole job, they will "beat a path"
to the shop featuring that type of work.

Toe tipping is very profitable for the material
used can be scraps of sole leather, corners from taps ,
etc.

Except in cases of welt type shoes attach toe tips by the cement method.

Toe tips can be put on men's shoes by the same methods as described below.

1.   Retipping - McKay and Cement
Type Shoes

A - Preparation of Shoe.

(1) Draw line across toe where tip is to be started. See Figure 124.

(Figure 124)

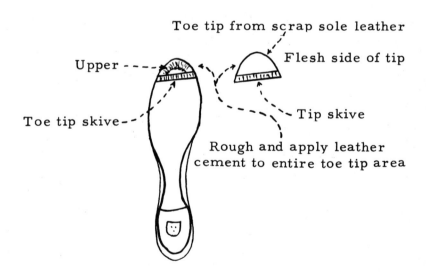

Toe tip from scrap sole leather

Upper

Flesh side of tip

Toe tip skive

Tip skive

Rough and apply leather cement to entire toe tip area

(2) Remove tips and skive from line the same as 1/2 soling operations. See Figure 125.

(Figure 125)

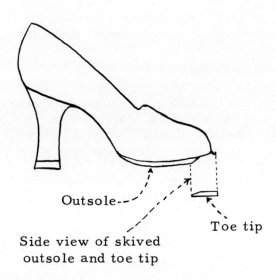

Outsole--

Toe tip

Side view of skived
outsole and toe tip

(3) Rough skive and balance off tip with
roughing tool.

(4) Apply thin coat of leather cement and
allow to dry.

B - Preparation of Tap.

(1) Skive butt of tip the same as tap butt.

(2) Rough entire tip with roughing tool.

(3) Apply thin coat of leather cement and allow to dry.

C - Attaching Tip.

(1) Apply second coat of leather cement to shoe.

(2) Place tip in position and fasten tempo-rarily with two lasting tacks.

(3) Fit press last in shoe the same as when cementing tap.

(4) Place shoe in shoe press as usual.

D - Finishing.

(1) Edge trim tip by same method as sole edge trimming.   It is recommended that the entire sole be edge trimmed to give tip invisible appearance.

(2) Scour bottom of tip so that there is a perfectly smooth surface at the joint with the sole.

(3) Edge set sole edge as usual.

2. - Retipping McKay and Cement Type
Shoes With Stapler.

A - Preparation of Shoe and Tip.

(1) Prepare shoe and tip the same as de-scribed above but for one exception. Apply rubber cement to shoe and tip instead of leather cement. Allow to dry.

B - Attaching Tip.

(1) Place tip in position and pound down to

insure joining of rubber cement on tip and shoe.

(2) Staple tip across butt and all around tip edge.

(3) Trim in usual manner.

C - Finishing.

(1) Edge trim, scour bottom and edge set the same as described in Paragraph 1-D, this chapter.

3. - Retipping Welt Type Shoe.

A - Prepare shoe and tip the same as method used in preparing welt shoe for half soling, cemented shank. Refer to Chapter 15, Paragraph 1.

B - Attaching Tip.

(1) Attach tip by same method as used for attaching half sole to welt type shoe. Refer to Chapter 15, Paragraph 1.

(2) After tip butt has been pressed, scour bottom making smooth joint between tip and shoe bottom.

(3) Stitch tip to welt on Goodyear Welt Stitcher.

C - Edge trim and edge set to finish as usual.

LESSON   19

A FEW WAYS TO RESOLE CHILDREN'S SHOES .

The majority of children's shoes are made by the stitchdown process.

Boy's and girls shoes are usually constructed either by the Goodyear Welt, Nailed or McKay processes. When resoling these shoes, follow the same operations as applied to men's or women's shoes made by the corresponding process.

As outlined previously, chrome tanned leather is a more wear resistant leather than Oak tanned, therefore it is recommended that Chrome leather be used on all children's; boy's and girl's shoes. Because of the hard wear the average child gives a pair of shoes it will be found that a large percentage of resole work in a shop is on children's shoes. By using the most wear resistant materials obtainable on children's shoes, an operator will make children's parents his friends. Remember that the parents wear shoes too.

1. - Resoling Stitchdown Shoes.

NOTE: There are a few men's and women's shoes made on the Stitchdown plan. They are resoled by the same process as outlined below.

A - Preparation of Shoe.

(1) If heel is to be replaced, remove it.

(2) Measure tap on shoe and draw line across shank as usual.

(3) Remove worn sole by cutting stitches between outsole and midsole.

(4) Skive shank as usual.

(5) If midsole is worn at edges or toe, "square up" worn parts, as outlined in Chapter 13, Paragraph 1-G.

(6) Check midsole to see if it fastened securely to upper. If midsole is loose at any place, cement it in place with rubber cement.

(7) With rasp or on sanding wheel, rough skive and midsole.

(8) Apply thin coat of rubber cement over entire roughened area. Allow cement to dry.

B - Preparation of tap. (Chrome Leather)

NOTE: If hard Oak leather is used, prepare tap as outlined in Chapter 6 ''Preparation of Soles''. Sole is then attached as outlined here for Chrome lea - ther.

(1) Chrome or retanned leather need not be tempered.

(2) Skive butt of tap as usual.

(3) With rasp, or on sanding wheel, rough entire flesh side of tap.

(4) Apply thin coat of rubber cement to tap. Allow to dry.

C - Attaching Tap.

(1) Place butt of tap in position at shank of shoe. Secure butt with nails or staples. With chrome leather use soling nails.   For children's shoes a double row of nails is recommended.

(2) Pound tap lightly over entire surface to insure tight joint between midsole and tap.

(3) With lip knife trim off excess leather of outsole. Trim outsole flush with midsole edge.

(4) With pincer press outsole and midsole edges together. Sole is now ready to be stitched.

(5) Stitchdown shoes are stitched on the Goodyear Welt Stitcher. Stitchdowns can be stitched on the regular needleplate (worktable) of the stitcher but it is recommended that a special Stitchdown Needle Plate be used. The Stitchdown Needle Plates are available from the stitcher manufacturer and it is a simple operation to change them on the machine. Manufacturer's Manual describes adjustment fully.

(6) Proceed to stitch sole the same as when stitching welt type shoes. Be sure to start and end stitching in back of tap butt. Care must be taken not to push shoe against needle-plate, this will cause shoe to be squeezed together. It is further recommended that stitchdown shoes be stitched at a slow rate of speed.

(7) Edge trim and edge set in the usual manner.

(8) When resoling Stitchdown shoes with full sole, from back of heel seat to toe, stitch completely around the shoe.

2. -   Attaching Sole to Stitchdown Shoe by
Stapling.

A - Shoe is prepared the same as outlined above.

B - Tap is prepared the same as above.

C - Attaching Tap.

(1) Same procedure is followed up to stitching sole.

(2) Instead of stitching, fasten sole by stapling.   When stapling, Stitchdown Shoe is held with bottom facing down. Staples are driven down through the top of welting and staples are clinched on top of tap. See Figure 126.

(Figure 126)

C u t a w a y   o f   S t i t c h d o w n   S h o e

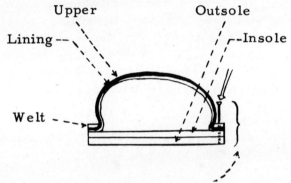

Upper   Outsole

Lining   --Insole

Welt

To attach outsole to stitchdown, other than stitching, drive nail or staple down from welt.

D - Sole edge is edge trimmed and edge set in the usual manner to finish.

LESSON   20

USEFUL   HINTS   ON   FIXING   HEELS

Heels for shoes are made of three different materials - - rubber, leather and wood.

Wood is used for heels on ladies shoes of all
types, but every wood heel has a layer (lift) of either
rubber or leather on the wearing surface.   Wood
heels are covered with either the same material as
the uppers or with celluloid of matching color.

Rubber and leather heels, either singly or combined are made for every type of shoe.   Rubber and leather heels are finished on the finishing machine to
attain color desired.

As mentioned earlier in this manual it is suggested that rubber heels be recommended to your customers whenever possible.   This is not only for their
good but also yours.   The benefits to the customer
have been mentioned before. For your benefit, rubber heels can be put on in a lot less time than leather
heels and the profit from both are about the same.

Unless the customer specifies differently it is
recommended that the operator reheel the shoe with
the same type of heel as originally on the shoe.

When a new heel has been put on a shoe, the shoe
should be set so that the entire wearing surface of the
heel and the ball of the sole are on a level plane. See
Figure 127. It will be noted that the thickness of the
heel at the breast is less than at the back of the heel.
This applies to all types and styles of heels.   See
Figure 127.

1. Rubber Heels: All rubber heels are constructed with a washer, or retainer, about midway in the
heel.   The washers are placed in line with the nail
holes and the heads of the nails are set into the
washers and in turn hold the heel secure to the shoe.
See Figure 128.

Practically all rubber heel manufacturers make

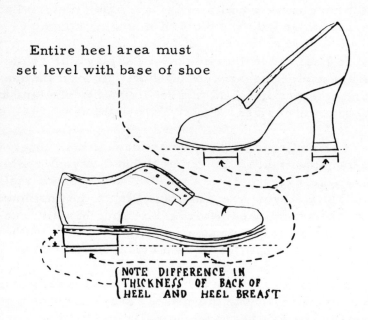

Entire heel area must
set level with base of shoe

NOTE DIFFERENCE IN
THICKNESS OF BACK OF
HEEL AND HEEL BREAST

Cutaway of Men's Goodyear Welt Shoe

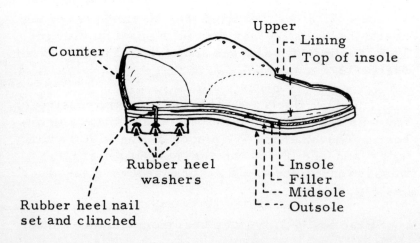

Counter

Upper
Lining
Top of insole

Rubber heel
washers

Insole
Filler
Midsole
Outsole

Rubber heel nail
set and clinched

three grades of heels. Use the grade of heel best suited for the type of business being conducted.   Again
it is strongly recommended that only first or best
quality materials be used.

Long   wearing   rubber   heels can be detected by
several tests but only two of the most common tests
will be described here.   First, place the heel in the
palms of the hand and attempt to close hand.   A long
wearing rubber heel will be fairly pliable.   Second,
hold the edge of the heel to the sanding wheel. If the
heel gives considerable resistance to sanding, it is
of good quality.

The materials used in quality heels is practically
all crude rubber while cheaper heels are made mostly
of reclaimed rubber and a carbon.

All styles and types of rubber heels are made in
brown and black.   In addition, women's Cuban and
Thin heels are made in white. Sport heels are made
in black, brown, red and white colors.

Following are descriptions of the standard types
of rubber heels:

A - Men's Whole Heel.

The men's whole rubber heel is about 7/8 of an
inch thick at the back and about 1/2 an inch thick at
the center of the breast.   Note that the bottom of the
heel is cupped to conform with the shape of the heel
seat of the shoe. The thickness of this heel is the
normal height for heels on men's shoes. See Figure
129.

B - Men's 1/2 Rubber Heels.

The 1/2 rubber heel is about one half an inch

Man's Whole Rubber Heel

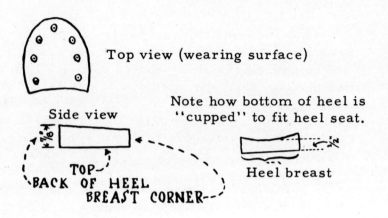

Top view (wearing surface)

Note how bottom of heel is "cupped" to fit heel seat.

Side view

TOP
BACK OF HEEL
BREAST CORNER

Heel breast

Men's 1/2 Rubber Heel

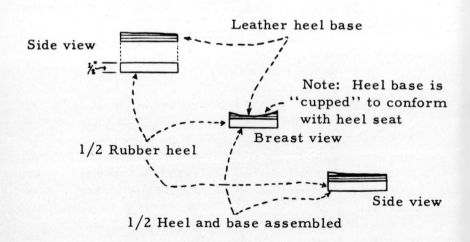

Leather heel base

Side view

Note: Heel base is "cupped" to conform with heel seat

Breast view

1/2 Rubber heel

Side view

1/2 Heel and base assembled

thick at the back. To bring the 1/2 heel up to normal height a heel base, usually made of leather, is secured to the shoe first and then the 1/2 heel is put on. The height of the combination is 7/8 of an inch at the back. As a rule the 1/2 heel combination is used on all men's dress shoes as it presents a dressier appearance. The bottom of the 1/2 heel is flat with a slight "lip" around the edge. See Figure 130.

C - Women's Cuban Rubber Heel.

The women's cuban heel looks similar to the men's 1/2 heel but it is only about 3/8 of an inch thick at the back. The bottom of the heel is flat. This heel is practically always used combined with a leather base. See Figure 131 below.

Woman's Cuban Heel

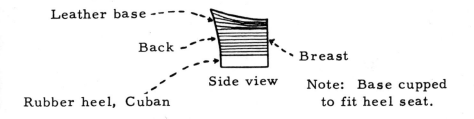

Leather base

Back

Breast

Side view

Rubber heel, Cuban

Note: Base cupped to fit heel seat.

RUBBER HEEL
LEATHER BASE

Top view   Breast view

D - Boy's and Girl's Whole Rubber Heel.

Boy's and Girl's whole heels are similar to Men's Whole Heels except that they are from 5/8 to 6/8 inches thick at the back according to the size.

E - Boy's and Girl's 1/2 Rubber Heel.

Boy's and Girl's 1/2 heels are the same as Women's Cuban Heels.

F - Ladies' Thin Rubber Heel.

Ladies' thin heels are about 3/16 of an inch thick, and are used as top lifts usually on wood heels. See Figure 132.

(Figure   132)

Woman's Thin Heel

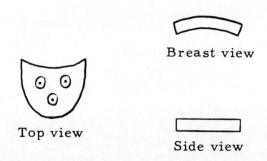

Breast view

Top view

Side view

G - Sport Heels.

Sport heels come in Men's, Women's and Children's sizes. They are usually the same thickness as whole heels in corresponding classes. The big difference between the whole heel and the sport heel

is the construction of the breast.   Whole heels are
straight up and down at the breast while the sport
heel tapers down to the shank. See Figure 133.

(Figure 133)

Rubber Sport Heel

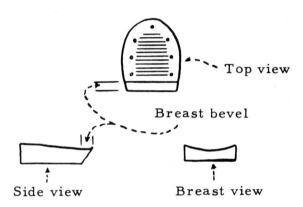

Top view

Breast bevel

Side view   Breast view

2.   Leather   Heels.

Leather heels, in the trade, are usually known
as built-up heels. They are thus named because they
are a succession of lifts (layers) of leather or "leather board" built one upon the other.   The first
few lifts from the base toward top are of either shoulder leather, belly leather or "leather board".   The
top lift is of hard prime leather usually 10 or 11 iron
in thickness.   The above applies to all leather heels
- - men's, women's and children's. Ready built-up
heels are available from jobbers in all standard shapes and sizes. See Figure 134.

NOTE: Leather board is a form of imitation leather.

A good percentage of people that wear leather

heels on their shoes wear a heel plate on top of the heel.   This is done to prolong the wear of the heel.

(Figure   134)

Leather Heels

Top views

Men's Leather Heels
(Also Women and
Children's Flat Heels)

Side
views

Breast
views

Woman's cuban

Woman's spike

Heel plates are made of metal and though there are a variety of designs the crescent type is the most popular. See Figure 134-A.

The crescent type heel plate comes in a variety of sizes.   The largest being about 3 inches across, to be used on men's shoes, to 3/8 of an inch across. The smaller plates are used on spike heels and on the toes of ladies shoes.   Many customers will request plates on both the heels and toes of their shoes. See Figure 134-A, next page.

(Figure 134-A)

Heel plates

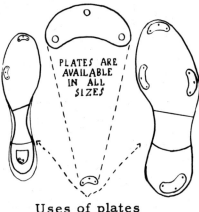

Uses of plates

The plates are punched with holes and nails are furnished with the plates for their use.

It is wise to carry a full line of sizes of plates at all times.   They are available from the jobbers.

3.   Wood   Heels.

Wood heels are used practically exclusively on women's shoes.   Wood heels are of three general types: cuban, spike and wedgies.   See Figure 135. As mentioned before, a top lift of either leather or rubber is used on the top of wood heels.

(Figure 135)

Wood Heels

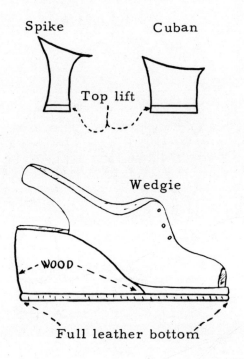

Spike

Cuban

Top lift

Wedgie

WOOD

Full leather bottom

All types and sizes of wood heels are available from jobbers.

LESSON XXI
SOME REHEELING TECHNIQUES

When reheeling all men's shoes and any other type shoe where nails will come through and clinch on the insole, remove old heel pad from inside shoe be- fore removing heel. Replace with new pad after fini- shing new heel.

A heel pad is a thin piece of leather, usually

sheepskin, and is used to cover up clinched nails of the heel.

(Figure 136)

Method For Removal Of Rubber Heel

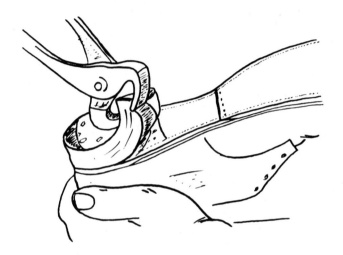

1. Reheeling with Rubber Heels.

A - Men's Whole Heel.

(1) Preparation of Shoe.

(a) Place shoe on last so that toe of shoe is pointed toward operator.

(b) Grasp counter of shoe with left hand and hold shoe firmly to the last. See Fig. 136.

(c) Grasp pincers with right hand. Grasp corner of heel with pincers and with a rolling motion "Peel" it off shoe away from operator. See Figure 136, page 153.

(d) Pull out remaining nails with pincers. See Figure 137, below.

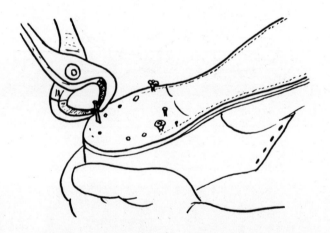

Method For Removal Of Heel Nails

(e) Fill old nail holes in heel seat with wood pegs. See Figure 138, next page.

(Figure 138)

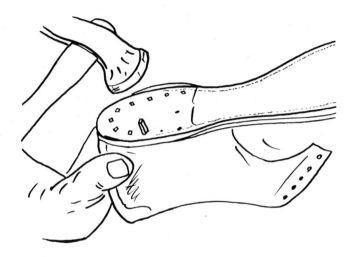

Filling Old Nail Holes With Wood Pegs

(f) Select size heel to fit heel seat.

(g) Rough bottom of heel and heel seat of shoe with rasp or on sanding wheel.

(h) Apply thin coat of rubber cement to both roughed surfaces. Allow cement to dry.

(2) Attaching Heel.

(a) Place back of heel flush with

back of heel seat. See Figure 139.

(Figure 139.)

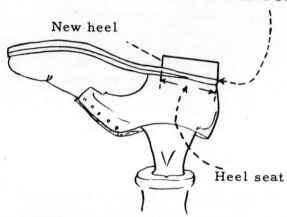

Place new heel with
its back flush with
back of heal seat

New heel

Heel seat

(b) Hold heel in position with left
hand. See Figure 140.

(c) Place rubber heel nail in back
nail hole. (Proper length of heel nails come with each
pair of heels).   Place nail so that it's point slants in
slightly toward center of shoe. See Figure 140. Drive
nail in as hard as possible.

Placing First Nail In New Heel

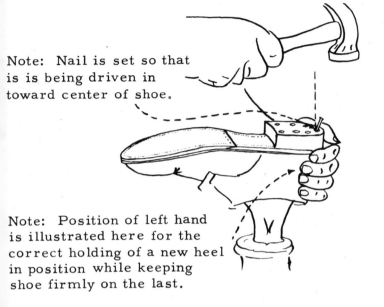

Note: Nail is set so that is is being driven in toward center of shoe.

Note: Position of left hand is illustrated here for the correct holding of a new heel in position while keeping shoe firmly on the last.

Setting Heel Nail With Nail Set

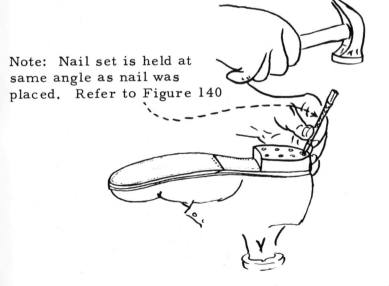

Note: Nail set is held at same angle as nail was placed. Refer to Figure 140

(d) Grasp nail set with left hand and hold set on nail just placed. With the aid of nail set drive nail down till it's head strikes washer in heel. Do not force nail further as washer will tear loose. See Figure 141.

(e) Place and set nails in two corners of nail holes. See Figure 142.

(f) Place and set nails in remaining nail holes. See Figure 142.

(Figure 142)
Sequence of Placing Nails In New Heel

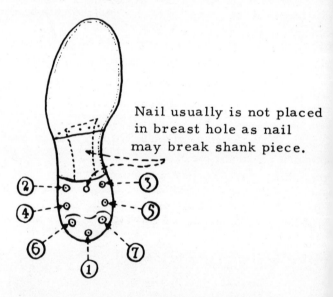

Nail usually is not placed in breast hole as nail may break shank piece.

(g) Remove shoe from last and with lip knife trim off excess rubber. Trim heel flush to heel seat. When trimming heel, shoe is held the same as for sole trimming.

(h) Heel is now ready to be finished. All rubber heels, except thin heels, are sanded smooth. Thin heels are trimmed on heel trimming blade attached to edge trimmer.

NOTE: The above operations apply to all types of rubber heels. Heel finishing is described in a separate lesson.

B -   Men's 1/2 and Women's Cuban Rubber Heels.

(1) Preparation of Shoe.

(a) Remove worn heel by same method as employed with whole heel.

(b) Remove remaining nails.

(c) Fill old nail holes with wood pegs.

(d) Check to see if heel base is level.   If base has been worn down at any place, sand worn edges on a bevel in such a manner that the bevel extends into heel about 3/4 of an inch. See Figure, 143.

(e) Build up bevel with skivings. Rubber cement and nail them in place - - until base is level. See Figure 143.

If the base of women's cuban heel is worn down beyond one lift replace worn lift. Be sure new lift is the same thickness as removed lift.

If the heel base on man's shoe is badly worn down or broken it is advisable to replace base. Ready made bases are available in all sizes from jobbers.

NOTE: The above "Squaring Up" operations apply if heel seat is worn down prior to attaching whole heel. The above operations also applies to heel bases of children's shoes.

(Figure 143)

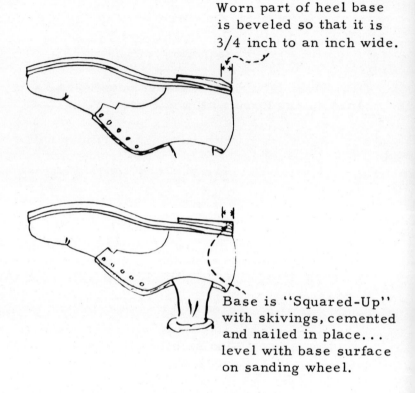

Worn part of heel base
is beveled so that it is
3/4 inch to an inch wide.

Base is "Squared-Up"
with skivings, cemented
and nailed in place...
level with base surface
on sanding wheel.

(f) Sand off heel base on bottom
sanding wheel so that it is level and clean.

(g) Heel bases of both shoes of the
pair must be the same height. Check before attaching rubber heels. See Figure 144. To check, hold
the pair of shoes, bottoms up, and the back of heels
flush. See Figure 144.

(h) Rough bottom of heel with rasp
or a sanding wheel.

(Figure 144)

Heel bases of pair
must be same height

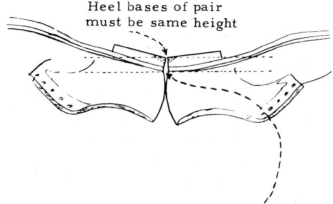

To check, hold mates
together - back to back -
heel seats together.

(i) Apply thin coat of rubber cement to both base and bottom of heel. Allow cement to dry.

(2) Attaching Heel.

Attach heel by the same method as for whole heel operations.

Heel is then ready for finishing operations. Heel finishing will be described in a separate chapter.

(3) Replacing With Leather.

A- Men's and Women's Cuban Heels.

NOTE: The following directions are for the removal and attaching of full built-up heel. As mentioned before, ready made built-up heels, with prime top lift, are available in all sizes and styles from jobber.

(1) Preparation of Shoe

(a) Remove old heel pads.

(b) Remove entire worn leather heel. There are two tools available for this job. (1) Hand Heel Remover; (2) Lever Type Heel Remover. (See Figure 145)

(Figure 145)

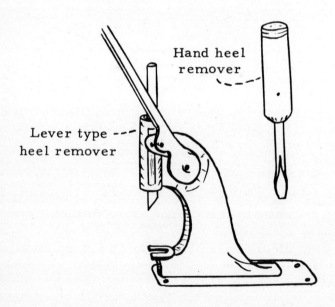

Hand heel remover

Lever type --- heel remover

(c) Removing heel with Hand Remover.

(I)   Place point of heel remover under bottom of heel at the breast and just in from the corner. See Figure 146.

(II)   Using Hammer, drive heel remover under heel about 3/4 to one inch. See Figure 146.

(Figure 146)

Removing Heel With
Hand Heel Remover

Heel remover

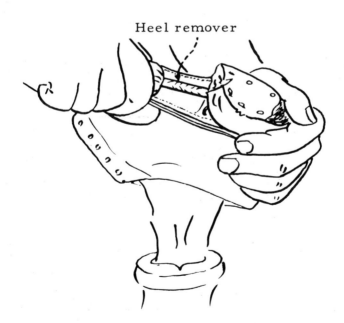

(III) Grasp handle of heel remover with right hand and force heel up and off. See Figure 146.

(IV) Pull out any remaining nails in heel seat.

(d) Removing heel with Lever Heel Remover.

(I) With right hand raise hand lever.

(II) Grasp upper of shoe with left hand. Place heel breast on breast plate of heel remover with the shoe facing operator. See Figure 147.

(III) Lower hand lever with right hand so that remover point strikes between joint of heel seat and heel bottom. See Figure 147.

(IV) Force lever down, thus dislodging heel.

(e) After heel has been removed pound heel seat thoroughly all around. This is done as heel seat may have come partially loose when heel was removed.

(f) Fill old nail holes with wood pegs.

(g) Select proper size and type of heel. (Men's or Women's).

(h) Rough heel seat and bottom of heel with rasp or on sanding machine.

(Figure 147)

Removing Heel With
Lever Type Remover

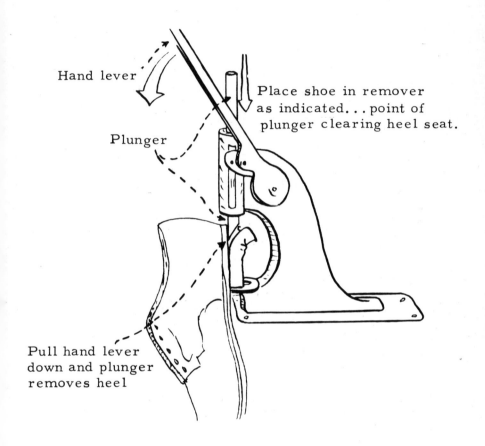

Hand lever

Place shoe in remover
as indicated...point of
plunger clearing heel seat.

Plunger

Pull hand lever
down and plunger
removes heel

(i)   Apply thin coat of rubber ce-
ment to heel seat and bottom of heel. Allow to dry.

(2) Attaching Heel.

(a)   Place heel on heel seat with
back of heel flush with back of heel seat. Refer to
Figure 139.

(b) With left hand hold shoe firmly on last and heel in place. Refer to Figure 139.

(c) Place square heeling nail at back of heel.   Nail should be set about 3/8 to 1/2 inch in from back edge. Drive nail in so that it just touches the last. See Figure 148.

(d) Cut off portion of nail sticking up and pound nail level with heel surface.

(e)   Place square heel nails at each corner. Place nails so that they are in about 1/2 inch from outside edges and about 1/2 inch in from heel breast. See Figure 148.

(f) Place two more square heel nails along each side of heel. Set nails so that they are the same distance in from edge as first three nails. See Figure 148. Set nails so that they are evenly spaced.

NOTE: It will be noted that the above operations are practically the same as attaching whole rubber heel.

(g)   Along the top of heel and where customer gives it the most wear, place a row of 5/8 or 6/8 clinching nails. These nails should be about 3/8 inch in from finished heel edge and evenly spaced. See Figure 149.

(h) Heel is now ready to be finished.

NOTE: Finished heel must be level on top and sit square with ball of sole. If top of heel has bumps on it, level off on bottom sanding wheel with same operation as scouring of sole bottom.

(Figure 148)

Attaching Leather Heel

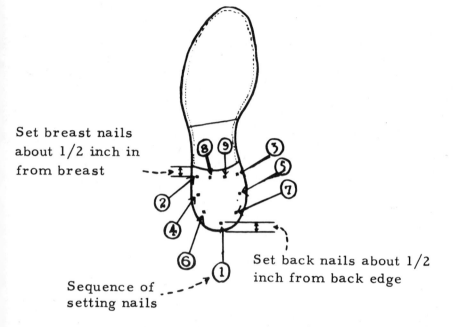

Set breast nails about 1/2 inch in from breast

Set back nails about 1/2 inch from back edge

Sequence of setting nails

B - Repairing Built-Up Heel. Men's and Women's.

(1) Remove top lift with hand heel remover. This is done by the same manner as removing entire heel.

(2) If heel is worn down beyond second lift, remove it.

(3) "Square-Up" next lift with skivings (wedge) cementing and nailing wedges in place.

(4) Level wedge with lift surface on bottom sanding wheel.

(**Figure** 149)

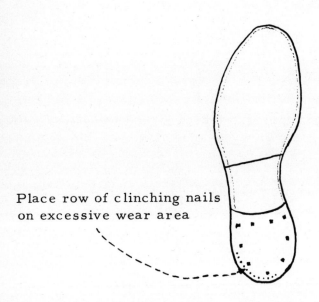

Place row of clinching nails
on excessive wear area

(5) Replace second lift with new lift
of same thickness as old second lift.

(6) Attach new top lift of prime leather
by cementing with rubber cement and nailing. Nail top
lift in same manner as described in Paragraph 2-A-(2),
this chapter. Refer to Figure 149.

(7) If heel is not worn down beyond sec-
ond lift, "square up" second lift as described above;
then attach top lift.

(8) With lip knife trim lift flush to base
of heel.

(9) Be sure that both heels of the pair
are the same shape and height. Check as in Figure 144.

(10) Heel is now ready for finishing.

3. Retipping Wood Heels.

    A. Spike and Cuban
        (1) Preparation of shoe.

            (a) With hand heel remover, re-
move worn top lift.

            (b) If heel covering is loose from
under lift, or is scuffed, or breasting is loose, cement
all in place with rubber cement. See Figure 150.

            (c) Heel is now ready for attach-
ing lift.

(Figure 150)

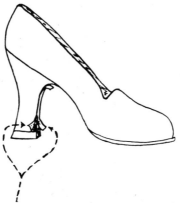

Loose heel covering and breasting

(d)If heel is worn down to the wood,
peel the covering down and sand wood heel level. See
Figure 151. Be sure to sand both of the pair down so
they are even.

(Figure 151)

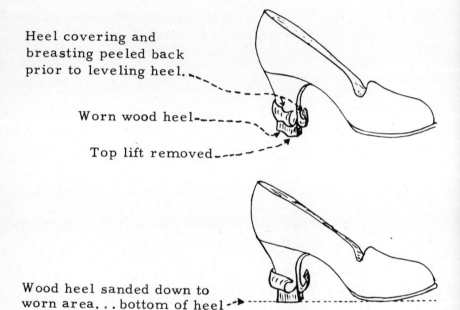

Heel covering and
breasting peeled back
prior to leveling heel.

Worn wood heel

Top lift removed

Wood heel sanded down to
worn area. . . bottom of heel
must set level with ball of shoe.
Both shoes of pair must be same height.

(e)Apply rubber cement to inside
of heel covering and to heel. Allow cement to dry.

(f) Pull up covering and stretch
so that there are no wrinkles. Lap covering over top of
heel with about 1/8 inch lap. See Figure 152.

(g)Heel is ready for attaching lift.

(Figure 152)

Bottom View Of Wood Heels

Cuban   Spike

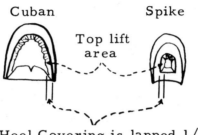

Heel Covering is lapped 1/8
inch over top lift area

        (2) Attaching lift (Leather or Rubber
Thin Heel).

        (a) Select lift of proper size.

        NOTE: Ready cut leather top lifts are
available in all sizes from jobbers. Top lifts can also
be cut from scraps of sole leather, corners of taps,
etc.   These lifts then are practically all profit. Be
sure that pieces selected for a pair are the same thickness.

        (b) Rough with rasp or on sand-
ing wheel bottom of top lift.

        (c) Apply rubber cement to heel
and bottom of top lift. Allow cement to dry.

(d) Hold shoe on last and top lift
in same manner as previous heeling operations.

(e) Use 5/8 or 6/8 wood heel nails
to attach lift.

(f)   Attach lift on spike heel with
three nails set in a triangular design. See Figure 153.
Place one nail toward center back of lift and the other
two towards breast corners. See Figure 153.

(Figure 153)

Attaching Top Lift

Sequence of setting
nails in top lift.

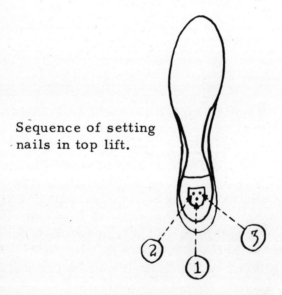

(g) On low wood heels use as many
nails as needed according to size of heel. Nails should
be set in about 3/16 inch from finished edge.

(h)   Drive nails into wood heels very carefully to avoid splitting heels.

NOTE: For those operators that possess a stapling machine, it should be used for attaching leather top lifts. Considerable time can be saved over the nailing method.

(i) Lift is now ready to be finished.

B-   Retipping Wedgies.

(1)   Preparation of Shoe

(a) Select size top lift that is wide enough for heel.

(b)   Place top lift on wedgie with back of lift flush with back of wedgie.   See Figure 154.   Draw line across wedgie at lift breast.   See Figure 154.

(c) Skive wedgie surface from line toward back of heel.   Skive to be 1/2 to 3/4 inch wide. Skive to feather edge.   See Figure 155.

(d) Skive breast of top lift to match wedgie skive.   See Figure 155.

(e)   Check covering on wedgie. Secure if loose.

(f) If wedgie is worn down, "square up" the same as leather built-up heel.

(g)   Rough bottom of lift.

(h)   Apply rubber cement to heel and bottom of lift.   Allow to dry.

(Figure 154)

When reheeling wedgies, place
back of proper size lift flush
with back of wedgie heel.

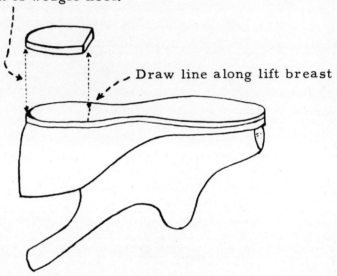

Draw line along lift breast

(2) Attaching Lift

(a) Place lift in position on wedgie and pound with hammer to insure adhesion.

(b) Scour heel lift level with shoe
bottom. Use same method as scouring tap butt for invisible 1/2 soling. Thus a level surface is attained on
wedgie as originally constructed.   See Figure 156.

(c) Nail top lift secure, using
wood heel nails. See Figure 157 for suggested nailing.
Lift is now ready for finishing.

(Figure 155)

Skive lift and wedgie heel to match

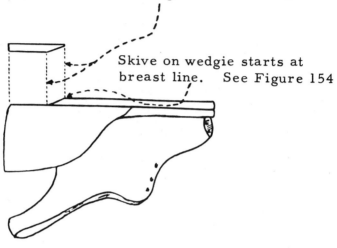

Skive on wedgie starts at
breast line.   See Figure 154

(Figure 156)

After attaching, new top lift is scoured
on level plane with wedgie bottom.

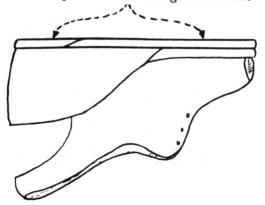

(Figure 157)

Wedgie bottom with suggested
nailing or stapling of top lift.

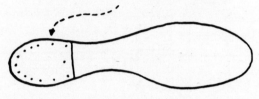

LESSON XXII

HOW TO FINISH HEELS

The finishing of heels consists of sanding smooth and
burnishing the edges of rubber and leather heels. The
edge trimming of leather top lifts and thin rubber heels
together with edge setting completes the finishing.

The finishing of heels is very important and a good
repair job can be made better or ruined by it.

When sanding heels be sure that the heel edge is entirely smooth - free of any ripples or bumps. This requires practice but it will be found that with a little patience you will soon be able to sand a heel perfectly
smooth with very little effort.

Men's heels are sanded on the flat, or "A" type,
sanding wheel. Women's heel are sanded on "B" type
sanding wheel. See Figure 158.

The breasts of men's and women's heels are made smooth on the heel breaster, a cone-shaped sanding wheel. The corners of the heels are made straight on the breaster also. See Figure 158.

(Figure 158)

Finisher Sanding Section

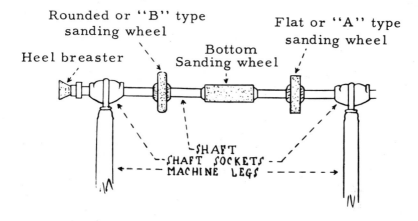

When shaping men's heels it is suggested that the in-side edge and back be straight up and down while the outer edge should flare out a trifle. See Figure 159. Check the shape of heels on new shoes and it will be found that the majority of them are shaped in that man-ner. The objective of every shoe repairman should al-ways be to repair shoes in such a way that they will have as much of a "like-new" appearance as possible. Also when shaping heels make corners of the heels straight.

(Figure 159)

Back View Of Man's Oxford

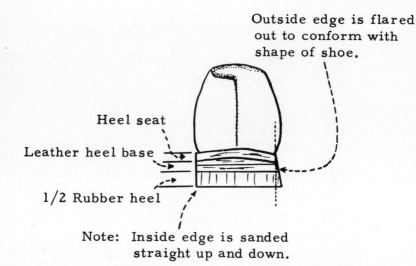

Outside edge is flared
out to conform with
shape of shoe.

Heel seat

Leather heel base

1/2 Rubber heel

Note: Inside edge is sanded
straight up and down.

When burnishing heel edges, practice to get a high gloss on them.   Do not leave a cloudy appearance on edges. Remember always, that a customer judges the workmanship of the repaired shoes by their final appearance.

A well finished job is a shop's best salesman.

1. SANDING MEN'S HEELS

A. Start sanding section in motion.

B. Grasp the counter of the shoe with the left hand and fingers of the right hand on the shank and against the heel breast.   The thumb of the right hand against the heel edges or counter. See Figure 160.

(Figure 160)

Heel Sanding

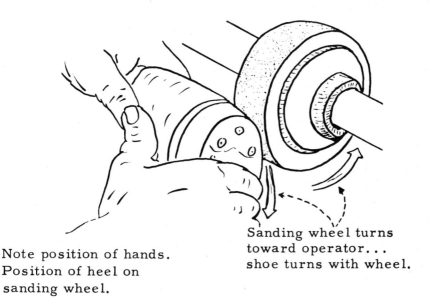

Note position of hands.
Position of heel on
sanding wheel.

Sanding wheel turns
toward operator...
shoe turns with wheel.

C. Place the corner of the heel, opposite from the operator, up to the front center of the sanding wheel. See Figure 160.

D.   Move the shoe around on the sanding wheel so that the heel is sanded from breast corner to breast corner in one continuous movement. See Figure 161. The shoe is held in the same manner throughout the entire movement, - it is merely a wrist action that swings the shoe around. See Figure 162. The action is the same as two cog wheels turning on each other. See Figure 161.   In order to insure a smooth surface on the heel edge it must be sanded in one movement.

(Figure 161)

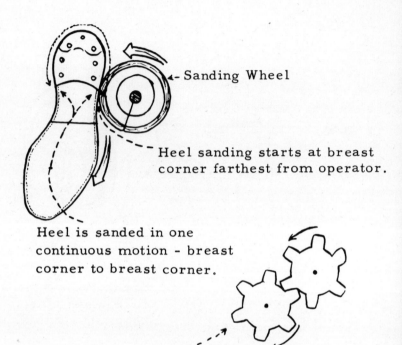

← Sanding Wheel

Heel sanding starts at breast
corner farthest from operator.

Heel is sanded in one
continuous motion - breast
corner to breast corner.

Heel turns with sanding wheel
the same as a cog-wheel operation.

   E.   Light, even pressure must be maintained all
the way around the heel edge.   Using too much pressure
will burn heel and cause discoloring.

   F.   The heel edge is sanded flush with the heel seat
edge.

   G.   Sanding wheel must not touch the shoe upper.
Sanding upper will cut it.

   H.   If heel edge is not sanded down enough on first
operation, continue to circle heel until sanded sufficient-
ly.

(Figure 162)

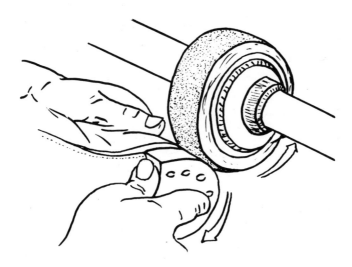

I.   To remove ripples or bumps on heel edge, circle heel edge very lightly on sanding wheel.

J.   To insure a perfect sanding job do the initial sanding on a coarse sandpaper -- 60 grit.   Then do final sanding on a fine sandpaper -- 0 or 00 grit.   In this manner the coarse paper is used to cut away excess material and shape heel.   Fine paper then removes any lines left by the coarse paper -- thus giving the heel a perfectly smooth edge.

K.   Next sand the heel breast on the breaster.   The shoe is held as shown in Figure 163.   The breast should be sanded in one movement -- heel corner to heel corner.   Follow the original contour of the breast when sanding. -- New whole rubber heels do not need to be sanded on the breaster.

NOTE: The above operations apply to both rubber and leather heels.

(Figure 163)

Sanding Heel Breast

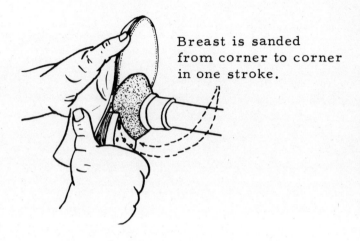

Breast is sanded
from corner to corner
in one stroke.

2. SANDING LADIES HEELS

A. As mentioned above, ladies' rubber and built-up
heels are sanded on "B" type sanding wheel. This is
done so that the heels may be shaped along original contour lines.

When shaping ladies heels do not change original
lines as the heel was designed to match the style of the
shoe. Remember the operator's job is to try to restore
a shoe, as near as possible, to its original appearance.

B. Hold the shoe in the same manner as when sanding men's heels.

C. Operations are identical as for sanding men's
heels.

D. It is suggested that when sanding ladies heels
to sand entire heel lightly to remove all stain. If all
the old stain is not removed the heel will finish off with
a two-toned effect.

3. TRIMMING WOOD HEEL LIFTS

A. Lifts are trimmed on special lift cutter attached on edge trimmer.

B. Shoe is held in same manner as for heel sanding operations.

C. Trim entire heel edge in one continuous movement as in heel sanding.

D. Lift breast is also trimmed on trimmer.

E. Trim lift edge to conform with heel contour.

4. HEEL BURNISHING

Burnishing is the process of applying burnishing ink to the raw edges, waxing the inked edges and then bringing wax to a high gloss.

Refer to Chapter 12, "Sole Burnishing" and Figure 86, "Close Up of Burnishing Section".

Remember that before using Burnishing ink, stir it thoroughly. Do not merely shake it. Stir it for the wax in the ink settles in the container and if the ink does not have its full consistency, a true color cannot be put on the edges.

A. Inking Heel Edges

(1) Grasp shoe upper with the left hand and hold shoe bottom up.

(2) With inking brush in right hand, apply burnishing ink to heel edges. Use same method as in Chapter 12, Paragraph 1. Do not allow ink to get on shoe upper or on bottom of heel.

(3) Allow ink to dry.

B. Heel Burnishing

(1) Set Burnishing Section in motion

(2) Grasp shoe in the same manner as when sanding heel.

(3) Hold heel edge up to front center of Burnishing Wheel. See Figure 164. Brush off dried ink in the same manner as when sanding heel. In other words, brush from heel corner to heel corner -- then back again. See Figure 165.

(4) Next hold heel edge to burnishing wheel in the same manner as when sanding heel. See Figure 166. Considerable pressure is needed to transfer wax from wheel to heel edge.

(5) Apply wax to entire heel surface from heel corner to heel corner in one complete movement. The wax must be applied evenly.

(6) As soon as wax is applied to heel edge take shoe back to burnishing brush.

(Figure 164)

Proper Method Of Holding Shoe
Up To Burnishing Brush

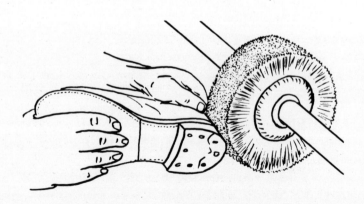

(Figure 165)

Heel Brushing

Burnishing brush

Same method is employed
for brushing heel as for
sanding. Heel is brushed
from breast corner to
breast corner in one
continuous stroke.

(Figure 166)

Heel Burnishing

Burnishing wheel

Heel is burnished
in the same manner
as in heel sanding.

Burnish entire heel
in one stroke.

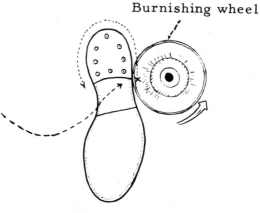

(7) Begin to brush heel again. This time heel should be circled six to eight times without removing heel from brush. On the first couple of rounds apply considerable pressure, and then gradually release until on the last couple of circling movements the heel edge is barely touching the brush. By this process the wax is heated and baked into the heel edge with the pressure strokes. For the lighter strokes will remove any cloudy appearances from the heel edge. The gloss is brought up by the lighter strokes.

Remember always - circle entire heel edge in one complete stroke for sanding, waxing, and brushing.

(8) Insert new heel pad on inside of shoe to cover clinched nails and to insure smooth surface for wearer's heel. Secure heel pad with rubber cement.

(9) Now check shoe upper for loose seams or holes.

C. Top Lift Burnishing

(1) Apply ink to lift edge in usual manner. Allow to dry.

(2) Brush off dry ink in usual manner.

(3) Apply lift edge to lift-setting wheel in same manner as when trimming same.

(4) Edge-set heel lift in one continuous movement. Considerable pressure is needed to set edge.

(5) Take shoe back to burnishing brush and brush lift edge lightly and in one movement.

LESSON XXIII

RECOMMENDED METHODS FOR REPAIRING RIPS AND PATCHES

Repairing rips and putting patches on shoe uppers is the most profitable part of the shoe repair business. This statement is made in view of the fact that aside from the investment of a Patching Machine the cost of this type of work is practically just your time.

As a craftsman, a shoe repairman's time is valuable but to place a high rate of value on a craftsman's time he must be skilled and above all neat.   This is especially true when repairing shoe uppers.

The reason the majority of people have shoes repaired is because of the comfort of a worn shoe, at the same time they want neat appearance.   Nothing spoils the appearance of a pair of shoes so much as a badly repaired upper.

Repairing rips or putting on patches are relatively simple operations, the main requirements are patience and neatness.

When charging the customer for these services the charge should be made on an hourly basis.   This charge should be based on prevailing local rates and need never be less than a minimum of 2 dollars per hour.   However many operators do not charge for repairing the rips on shoes that receive a reheel and resole job also.   It is considered good business to give this added service on a complete job.   The average customer will notice and appreciate the added free service.

Rips and Patches can be done by two different methods -- (1) Cementing; (2) Sewing.

One thing to remember when repairing any upper seam -- always remove the old stitches before repairing.

Whenever possible it is recommended that the Cement method be used.   The Cement Method requires a little more time but a neater and longer lasting job can be done.

Cementing is done by using Leather Celluloid Cement thinned down to about half it's regular consistency.   The cement is thinned with Celluloid Cement Thinner.

Sewing is done on what is known as a Shoe Patching Machine. The Patching Machine in practically all respects is like an ordinary home sewing machine. See Figure 167. The principle is the same in that two threads are employed to make a stitch.   One thread is wound through the machine and the other in a bobbin. The main difference is that the Patching Machine has an Arm for the work to rest on while a house sewing machine has a table. See Figure 167. Portable tables are available and can be attached to fit around the Arm of the Patching Machine.

(Figure 167)

Singer Patching Machine

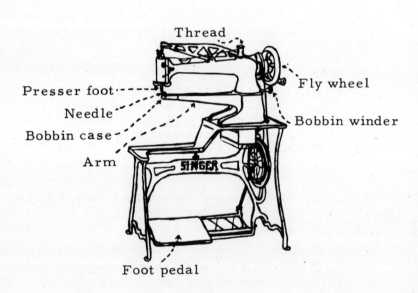

There are several makes and models of patching machines on the market. Figure 167 illustrates one model.

A variety of sizes of needles are available for the patching machine. Use the size needle best suited for the type material to be sewed. In other words, the heavier the leather to be sewed, the heavier needle that will be needed.

A variety of thicknesses of threads are available. Be sure to use a size thread to correspond to the size needle being used. Manufacturer's Manual will give the correct thread to use with each size needle.

Thread is also available in linen, cotton and silk and in all colors. Use color and type thread to match material being sewed.

Scraps of new upper leathers can be obtained from jobbers at very little cost. Keep an assorted supply on hand at all times so that any shoe can be patched correctly.

1. Cement Method
　　A. -- Rips
　　　　(1) Remove old stitches.
　　　　(2) With leather cement thinner clean and soften the surfaces of the parts to be repaired. See Figure 168.
　　　　(3) With a piece of sandpaper, rough surfaces to be united. See Figure 168.
　　　　(4) Apply coat of thinned leather cement to roughened surfaces. Allow to dry. See Figure 168.
　　　　(5) Apply second coat of thinned cement to surfaces. Place surfaces in position. With the hands, hold surfaces in place until cement has dried. If possible, place a few small lasting tacks along seam and they will act as a press.
　　　　(6) After cement has dried remove tacks and seam is repaired.

(Figure 168)

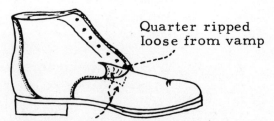

Quarter ripped
loose from vamp

Old stitch line...area to be
cleaned and roughed prior to
applying leather cement.

B. --Patches

(1) Trim edges evenly of hole to be patched.
See Figure 169.

(2) Clean under side of hole edges with thinner.

(3) Rough under side of hole edges.

(4) Apply coat of thinned leather cement to
roughed surface.

(5) Cut patch from leather matching upper
to be repaired. Cut patch so that it will extend over
hole about 1/4 inch on all sides.

(6) Skive to a feather edge the 1/4 inch ex-
tension of the patch. See Figure 169.

(7) Rough skived edge of patch.

(8) Apply coat of thinned leather cement to
shived portion. Allow to dry.

(9) Apply second coat of leather cement to
both surfaces and place patch on the inside of shoe and
in the hole. See Figure 169. Hold the patch in place
with the hands until cement has dried. Shoe stretcher
may be inserted inside shoe and turned up just enough
to hold patch tight to upper until dry. Remove stretcher.
See Figure 170. By this manner an invisible and com-
fortable patch will be made.

(Figure 169)

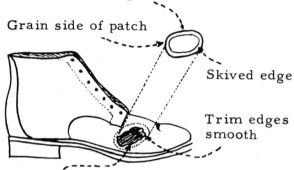

Replacement Patch - About
1/2 Inch Larger Than Hole

Grain side of patch

Skived edge

Trim edges
smooth

Clean and rough indicated
area on inside of upper

(Figure 170)

Shoe Stretcher

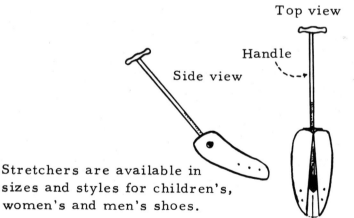

Top view

Handle

Side view

Stretchers are available in
sizes and styles for children's,
women's and men's shoes.

Shoe is stretched by turning handle
which spreads and retracts wings.

(10) Replacing Back Stay

(a) To remove worn back stay remove heel and loosen back of heel seat. See Figure 171.

(Figure 171)

Back View Of Shoe

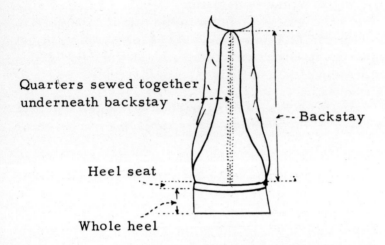

Quarters sewed together underneath backstay

Backstay

Heel seat

Whole heel

(b) If stitches holding the two quarters together are broken, stitch by hand.

(c) Cut new back stay, using old one as pattern.

(d) Rough surface of upper to be covered by back stay and flesh side of new back stay.

(e) Apply coat of thinned leather cement to roughed surfaces. Allow to dry.

(f) Apply second coat of cement to back stay and upper. Put back stay in position and secure with a few lasting tacks.

(g) After cement has dried, remove tacks. Tuck bottom end of back stay under loosened heel seat. Nail heel seat in place and replace heel.

The cement method is recommended for replacing back stays because of the difficulty in sewing through counter of shoe.

2. Sewing

   (A) Rips

        (1) Remove old stitches from loose seams.

        (2) Rough surfaces, to be sewed, with sand-paper.

        (3) Apply thin coat of rubber cement to rough-ed surfaces. Allow to dry.

        (4) Place surfaces in position. Proceed to sew, with patching machine, prepared seam. Adjust machine so it will sew in the old stitch holes. The Manufacturers' Manual gives full instructions for all adjustments.

        (5) When placing ripped surfaces together place them in their original positions.

   (B) Patches

        (1) Patches may be attached either on the inside or outside of shoe by sewing.

        (2) Prepare patch and shoe the same as for the Cement Method. There is one exception--apply rubber cement instead of leather cement.

        (3) After cement has dried place patch over hole. Sew around the patch with patching machine. Make seam with an even row of stitches. To insure even row of stitching, draw a line where the stitches are to be. Then follow line.   It is suggested that on heavy shoes two rows of stitches always be used.   On dress shoes use only a single row.

LESSON XXIIII

HOW TO REWELT SHOES

As a rule shoe repairmen of today replace worn pieces of welt by sewing the new welt to the insole with a McKay Stitcher or fasten it with a stapling machine. Old timers use the waxed-end method -- sewing welt by hand.

For repair work either method is acceptable, but for the better job the wax-end method is preferable, although it is considerably slower.

Welting can be obtained from jobbers in sizes for both men and womens' shoes. See Figure 172.

(Figure 172)

Welt

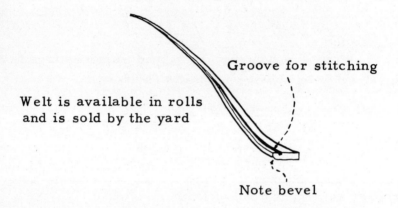

Groove for stitching

Welt is available in rolls
and is sold by the yard

Note bevel

1. MACHINE METHOD

A.   Remove worn part of welt by cutting stitches of inseam. See Figure 173.

B.   Skive remaining welt end at about a 3/8 of an inch skive. See Figure 173.

C.   Cut and skive new welt to fit in worn welt space.

D.. Holding new welt in place in inseam proceed to fasten welt to shoe with either McKay Stitches or stapling machine. The welt will be fastened in such manner that the stitches (or staples) will fasten the welt to the insole instead of insole rib as originally. See Figure 174.

E.   With lip knife trim new welting to correspond, in width, with old welt.

(Figure 173)

Bottom Of Welt Shoe

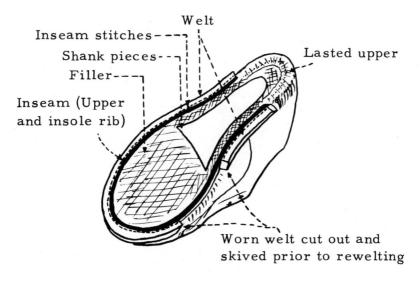

Welt

Inseam stitches

Shank pieces

Filler

Inseam (Upper
and insole rib)

Lasted upper

Worn welt cut out and
skived prior to rewelting

(Figure 174)

Cutaway Of Welt Shoe

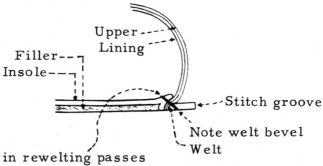

Upper

Lining

Filler

Insole

Stitch groove

Note welt bevel

Welt

McKay stitch in rewelting passes
through welt, upper, and insole.

2. WAXED-END METHOD

    A. Making the wax-end

       (1) Wax-ends are made from Irish Flax sometimes known as "Shoemakers Thread."

       (2) Lay thread over right thigh with a few inches hanging over leg.

       (3) Grasp end of thread with left hand.

       (4) Place palm of right hand on thigh, over thread, and rub hand downward, causing thread to untwist.

       (5) With thumb and forefinger of right hand, grasp thread about 8 or 10 inches from the end. (End of thread is still being held by left hand.) Pull with both hands, causing thread to pull apart so that the thread has a tapering end.

       (6) Measure out about two yards of the thread and break in the same manner described above. Therefore, both ends of thread will be tapered.

       (7) Measure out another so that it is about 3 or 4 inches shorter than the first strand. Taper ends in the same manner.

       (8) Measure out third strand about 4 inches shorter than the second.

    NOTE: For light sewing, three strands are sufficient. If stronger thread will be needed, measure out three more strands in corresponding lengths to the first three so that you will have two of each length. For sewing ladies welt three strand thread is sufficient. For mens' welt use six strand.

       (9) Hang all strands, at their center, over nail or hook. See Figure 175.

       (10) Apply shoemaker's wax to end for about 6 to 8 inches.

       (11) Take one set of ends and twist. Twisting is done by placing ends on thigh, place right hand over ends and rub ends down thigh causing ends to twist together. Rub end several times to twist end thoroughly. --Always rub down thigh--when knee is reached, pick thread up and start at top of thigh again. Do not rub up and down thigh as thread will not twist.

(Figure 175)

Strands Of Shoemaker's Thread Prior To
Waxing And Twisting Into Wax-End

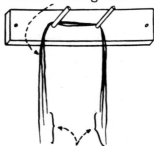

Apply shoemaker's wax to strand
ends then twist each series of ends.

(12) Twist second end in same manner.   Ends
will now be in a long point of about 6 inches long.

(13) Twist balance of strands forming strands
into one thread.

(14) Wax balance of thread by rubbing shoemaker's wax over it thoroughly several times.

(15) Thread about 4 inches of end through eye
of bristle. Turn thread back and twist into thread. See
Figure 176. Repeat operation on opposite end. Wax-end
is now ready for sewing.

B.   Sewing welt with wax-end

(1)   Place shoe on last.

(2)   Remove portion of worn welt, to be replaced, by cutting stitches of inseam.

(3)   Make about 3/8 inch skive on ends of
welt remaining on shoe.   Refer to Figure 173.

(4)   Cut and skive new welting to fit in section to be rewelted.

(5)   Remove old stitches from inseam from
section to be rewelted.

(6)   Set new strip of welting in position.

(7)   Make hole through inseam, with curved
awl, about 1/4 inch in back of end of old welt. See
Figure 177.

(Figure 176)

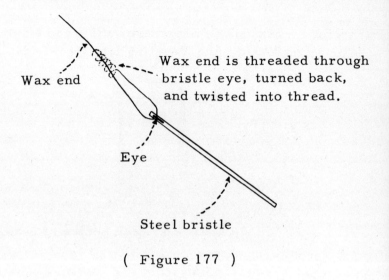

Wax end

Wax end is threaded through
bristle eye, turned back,
and twisted into thread.

Eye

Steel bristle

(Figure 177)

Cutaway Of Welt Shoe

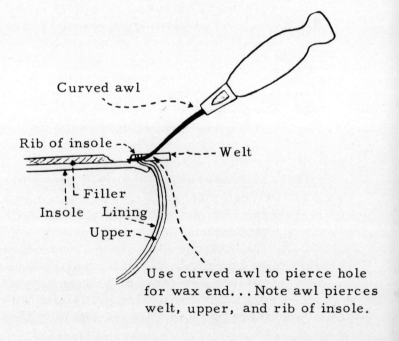

Curved awl

Rib of insole

Welt

Filler

Insole   Lining

Upper

Use curved awl to pierce hole
for wax end... Note awl pierces
welt, upper, and rib of insole.

(8) Insert one end of wax-end in hole. Draw thread through hole until same amount of thread extends on each side of inseam.

(9) Make second hole through inseam and end of new welt strip.

(10) Insert both ends of wax-end into second hole from opposite sides. (See Figure 178)

(Figure 178)

Cutaway Of Welt Shoe

Opposite ends of wax-end are pulled through inseam hole at the same time. The inseam hole is made with a curved awl - see Figure 177.

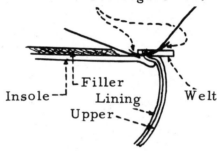

Insole   Filler   Lining   Upper   Welt

(11) Pull thread as tight as possible from both sides, forming stitch. (See Figure 179)

(12) Continue operations of (9), (10), (11) for the distance of the new welt using old inseam stitch holes as guide. Stitches will be about 1/4 inch in length. (See Figure 179)

(13) Continue stitches to the point where end stitch will come into old welt.

(14) To make last stitch, pass outside thread through hole to inside -- tie two ends together so that knot lays next to lip of insole. (See Figure 179)

(15) Cut off remaining threads. Tie cut ends together and wax-end is ready for use again.

(16) Tap new welt and inseam lightly with hammer to aid in setting stitches.

(17) With lip knife trim new welt to correspond, in width, with the old. Shoe is now ready to prepare for stitching on tap.

(Figure 179)

Bottom Of Welt Shoe

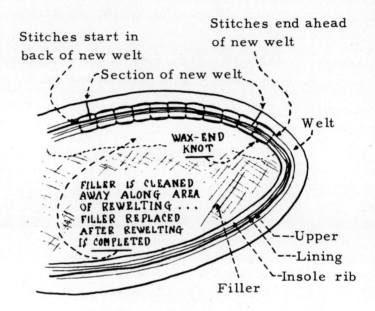

LESSON   XXV

HOW SHOES MAY BE REPAIRED
WITHOUT MACHINERY

Repairing shoes entirely without machinery is not recommended for commercial purposes. It is merely being outlined here briefly to show the student how shoes could be repaired with just hand tools, a piece of glass and a jack. Soles can be put on any type of shoe by nailing, so the following directions can apply.

1.   Preparation of Shoe

    A. Fit tap on shoe and draw line across the shank in usual manner.

    B. Remove sole in usual manner.

    C. Skive shank.

    D. Rough shank and shoe bottom with rasp.

    E. Apply rubber cement to roughed surface. Allow to dry.

2.   Preparation of Tap

    A.   Skive tap butt with straight or skiving knife as shown in Figure 28.

    B.   Rough flesh side of tap with rasp.

    C.   Apply thin coat of rubber cement to roughened surface. Allow to dry.

    D.   Temper tap as usual.

3.   Attaching of Tap

    A. Attach tap by same method as outlined in Chapter No. 16, "Resoling Men's Nailed Shoes".

4.   Finishing Sole Edges

    A. When trimming sole edge with lip knife, trim edge as smooth as possible.

    B. Then, with either a piece of sandpaper tacked on block of wood, about 2 inches wide and 4 to 6 inches long, or with a piece of glass rub sole edge smooth.

    C. Apply burnishing ink to edge in usual manner. Allow to dry.

    D. With a bristle shine brush, brush off dry ink.

    E. Apply paste polish to sole edge.

    F. With bristle shine brush shine sole edge.

NOTE: On welt type shoe, sole may be sewed on by using wax-end.   Use the same method and stitch in sewing sole to welt, as outlined in Chapter No. 24, "Rewelting Shoe".

5. Reheeling

      A. Follow same operations as outlined in Chapter No. 21, "Reheeling".

      B. Finish heels in the same manner as outlined in Paragraph 4 above.

LESSON   XXVI

BEST WAYS TO CARE FOR SHOES

You, as a shoe repairman, will be expected to know proper methods for the care of shoes and other leather items. It will be to your advantage to be able to give this advice to your customers.

Individual materials of course require special care adaptable to each material. In this chapter methods of the cleaning and preservation of popular types of shoes and leather goods will be given.

There are on the market hundreds of cleaning agents for shoes. In spite of the number of brands, shoe cleaning agents consist of nine general types and four types of brushes.

1. POLISHES

      A- Paste Polish - in a variety of standard colors for all smooth leathers.

      (1) Gloss Polish - a variation of paste polish. Comes in all standard colors but contains very little color pigment. Used after regular paste polish to give added gloss and for hardening surface. Aids in giving a lasting shine.

      B- Liquid Polish -   comes in all standard colors for smooth leather shoes. Does not need brushing to bring up shine.

C - Saddle Soap - is colorless and is used for cleaning all types of smooth leather shoes and all leather items except suede and buck leather. It cleans, softens and preserves leather. Can be brushed up to a gloss.

D - White Cleaners
    (1) Liquid
    (2) Cream
    (3) Cake

The above three are all used for cleaning all white shoes and white leather items. The difference is merely in their form.

E - Suede Cleaners
    (1) Liquid
    (2) Powder

Both of the above are for cleaning and renewing the color of suede and buck leathers. They are available in all colors.

F - Leather Renewers - Comes in liquid form. Pigment coloring does not penetrate the leather but restores an even color to the shoe. Especially popular for school shoes and badly scuffed shoes. Available in all colors.

G - Cleaning Fluid - Is colorless and is used for cleaning cloth shoes and removing spots on leather shoes. Also is used for cleaning suede and buck leathers before applying suede cleaners. Strictly a cleaner.

H - Shoe Creams - Is a shoe polish in cream form. Is available in all colors and contains a high polish property. Cream polishes are especially adaptable for soft leathers. Shoe creams come in either bottles or tubes depended upon the manufacture.

I - Oils and Greases
    (1) Neatsfoot Oil - This is the best type of leather softner and preserver. Is also used on shoes and boots to aid in waterproofing same. It is not recommended for use on any type of shoes that are to be shined. Oil will prevent attaining a gloss on the leather.
    (2) Greases - Are just another form of leather oils.

2. BRUSHES - Brushes come under two general classifications namely;application and shining brushes.

(1) Application type, known as daubers and are used for applying paste polish to shoes. (See Figure 180)

(2) Polishing types, known as shine brushes and are used to brush shoes after polish has been applied. There are three types; hair bristle brush, wool brush and suede brush. Soft wool shine cloth can be used in place of wool brush.

Suede brushes are made of stiff hair bristles, rubber bristles or wire bristles. Suede brushes are small in size and are used to brush up the nap on suede and buckskin leathers after polishes have been applied. (See Figure 180)

(Figure 180)

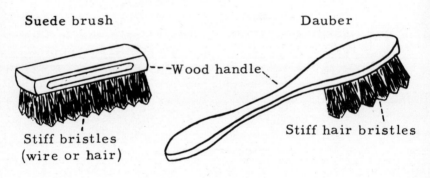

Suede brush   Dauber

---Wood handle

Stiff bristles   Stiff hair bristles
(wire or hair)

Shine Brushes

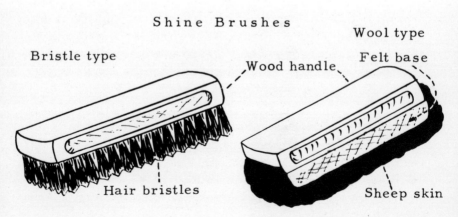

Wool type

Bristle type   Felt base

Wood handle

Hair bristles   Sheep skin

3. WET SHOES

When leather shoes have become wet, shoe trees should be inserted into the shoes as soon as they have been removed from the feet of the wearer. This is done to prevent shoes from shrinking while drying and also to help them to dry straight. If shoe trees are not available stuff the shoes with paper.

Do not set shoes near heating equipment, of any type, to dry. Let them dry normally with the room temperature. When shoes are dry, shine them with an oil-base type of shoe polish. If the shoes are work shoes, apply a coat of good grade Neatsfoot Oil.

NOTE: Neatsfoot Oil is made primarily for softening and preserving leather.

4. IDLE SHOES

When shoes are not to be worn for any length of time, insert shoe trees in them. This will enable shoes to dry out and while drying out avoid the uppers from shrinking and the shoe from curling up. Practically all shoes become slightly damp on the inside, from perspiration, while being worn.

After shoe trees have been inserted, wipe dust off the shoes with a soft wool brush or soft cloth. If shoes are made of suede leather, brush with regular suede brush or any stiff bristle brush. After shoes are dusted place them in Shoe Mitts. Thus shoes will be held straight and dust will not settle in the pores of the leather.

In the case of seasonable shoes that the owner wishes to put away for some time, and shoe trees are not available, stuff shoes with paper.

5. SHINING SMOOTH LEATHER SHOES

The secret of a good, lasting shine is the proper cleaning of the shoes before applying polish. The following directions may be followed when shining shoes on a Shine Chair.

Saddle Soap is one of the best cleaning agents for leather. Saddle Soap not only cleans but softens leather. It is especially adaptable for leather items that may come in contact with clothing.

A- Clean off any dried mud with a piece of wood or stiff bristle brush. Never use a knife. Be sure that top of welt and edges of other seams are free of all dirt.

B- Brush off entire shoe with bristle shine brush.

C- Wash shoe thoroughly with saddle soap.

D- Dry shoe first with absorbent cloth. Next, brush shoe dry with bristle shine brush.

E- If old polish or gummed material remains on shoe, clean shoe with a light application of a clear cleaning fluid.

F- With dauber, apply a thin coat of paste polish to shoe. Work polish into leather thoroughly. Do not apply lots of polish to shoe for it will result in a dull shine and in time will cause shoe to crack. Do not apply polish with fingers as body oils will cause spots on any color shoe except black.

G- Brush entire shoe thoroughly with bristle shine brush.

H- Apply thin coat of a gloss polish. This type of polish is made especially for hardening surface, bringing up better gloss and contains very little coloring.

I- Brush thoroughly with bristle shine brush.

J- Apply thin coat of neutral lotion cream over shoe.

K- Brush thoroughly with bristle shine brush.

L- Next rub shoe lightly with a soft wool shine cloth or wool type shine brush. The result will be a very glossy and lasting shine.

M- With inking brush apply edge-ink to sole and heel edges. Do not allow edge-ink to touch the uppers. Edge inks are made especially for this purpose.

6.   CLEANING WHITE SMOOTH LEATHER SHOES

A- Remove laces

B- Insert shoe trees or stuff shoes with paper.

C- Wash shoes and laces thoroughly with good quality toilet soap and water with brush. Be sure to remove all old polish.

D- Allow shoes to dry normally.

E- Apply white polish according to directions for type of polish being used. Manufacturer's directions are with each unit of polish.

F- Allow polish to dry.

G- Brush shoes lightly with wool shine brush or shine cloth.

H- With inking brush apply brown edge-ink to edges of sole and top lift of heel.

I- Press (with hot iron) and insert laces.

J- On white Buckskin shoes (leather with short nap similar to suede) after polish has dried, brush up nap with a suede or stiff bristle brush.   Work brush in a small circular motion to raise nap.

7.   CLEANING   TWO-TONED WHITE SHOES
(Combinations of White and Colored Leathers)

A- Clean entire shoe as described for white shoes. Allow to dry.

B- Apply white polish to white portion of shoe. Allow to dry.

C- Apply liquid polish to colored portion of shoe. Allow to dry.

D- Brush shoe as described for white shoes.

E- Apply edge-ink, using same color as originally used on edges.

8.   CLEANING SUEDE SHOES

A- With Suede Brush remove dust and other particles that may be in the nap. When brushing suede shoes always work brush in small circular motion.

B- Remove gum or any other sticky substance with fine grit sandpaper. Rub spots lightly and in a circular motion with the sandpaper.

C - Apply cleaning fluid rubbing it in with a circular motion. Allow to dry.

D - Apply Suede Dressing (polish) with dauber. Work dauber in circular motion to get the dressing on both sides of the nap.

E - While dressing is still wet on shoe, bring up nap with suede brush. Work brush in circular motion.

F - Allow dressing to dry after bringing up the nap.

G - Apply edge-ink

9. OILING WORK-TYPE SHOES AND BOOTS

A - Insert shoe trees, or stuff shoes with paper.

B - Wash shoes (or boots) thoroughly with Saddle Soap. Allow to dry.

C - With dauber apply a good grade neatsfoot oil or shoe grease to shoe. Work it into the leather thoroughly.

D - Allow shoe to sit for at least 12 hours before wearing.

10. CLEANING LEATHER GOODS

When cleaning different types of leather goods such as purses, wallets, leather jackets, etc., use only saddle soap. The use of dressings or polishes on items that may come in contact with clothing is not recommended as practically all dressings will either rub off on clothing or stain.

For cleaning suede jackets practically all Dry Cleaning establishments have a special solution they use in cleaning of suede jackets. It is recommended that this type of jacket be given to them to clean.

LESSON XXVII

HOW TO ARRANGE YOUR SHOP EFFECTIVELY

Shoe repair shops in the past have often been in out-of-the-way locations with little thought given to either customer appeal or operators' convenience.

As a result, the shoe repair industry, as a whole, went steadily down hill in every respect. After careful research, it was found that all that was wrong with the industry was that it had let itself die a slow miserable death. With the research, experiments were tried and it was found that all the industry needed was modernization. It was found that if the shoe repair business was conducted along the same lines as other businesses it would flourish and prosper.

The size and shape of a shoe shop location are not as important as for other businesses. This is due to the fact that the equipment necessary for shoe repairing is such that there is practically no standard arrangement.

There are three things that must be kept in mind when setting up a shop. The three items are (1) Location (2) Interior Arrangement (3) Working Convenience.

1.   Location
        Get where the "foot-traffic" is. As a rule, people nowadays do not come to you unless you are handy to them. Today one gets business only by being in people's way.
        Set up where people are and make your store attractive to them. Just being in their way won't do it all.
        Keep the front of your shop clean and attractive at all times. Keep your window trimmed attractively and change displays every 10 days to two weeks at the most. This will do more to attract attention than anything else.
        If your shop is neat and attractive from the outside, people unconsciously feel that you are neat about your work and that you are naturally particular.
        Due to the fact that a shoe repair business does not require too much space good small locations can usually be secured in the heart of traffic.

Many operators lease a portion of a floor of a big or popular department store. This has it's advantages for the popularity of the store brings people to your section.

2. Interior Arrangement

Plan your shop so that your customers have to walk past your accessory displays. Have it so planned that they will go past your accessories not only when they come in but also when they go out.

People buy more merchandise because of what they see than for any other reason. In order to sell an item, put it out in front of them--literally make them trip over what you have to sell.

When featuring "While You Wait" Service have booths, or waiting chairs, so placed that the customer has to look at your accessory displays while they are waiting.

Have the interior of the shop decorated in light colors. Have the shop well lighted at all times--make it look alert and alive.

3. Working Convenience

The work shop should be as handy as it is possible to make it. Try to have machinery and materials arranged so everything is practically at your finger-tips. The less steps the operator has to make the quicker each job can be turned out. The amount of your profit will be governed, naturally, by the number of jobs turned out and the amount of accessories sold.

Figure 181 gives the floor plan of a one-man shop that proved very successful. Of late years many one and two-men shops have used this plan as a model, varying it according to size and shape of building used. In every instance it has proved successful especially when the operator cooperated by doing his bit. By cooperation it is meant that the operator kept both the outside and inside of the shop clean and attractive. He gave good quality of workmanship and quick, courteous service.

He kept up his stocks of materials and accessories and made himself popular in community affairs.

The shop illustrated in Figure 181 was located next door to a popular theater and on a street with lots of foot traffic both day and night.

Due to the fact that the shop was next door to a theater the operator spent the bulk of his advertising budget on window display.

Due to the size of the building it was easy to lease as it was too small for the average of other types of business. The overall size of the building was 16 feet by 44 feet. The building was so constructed that it had a permanent partition across the center of it which also made it less attractive for the average business. As mentioned before shoe repair equipment is flexible as to arrangement so that even though the location was very desirable for business yet it restricted most business because of its physical set up.

Study Figure 181 and it will be found that using its general plan a shop can be set up in practically any shape building.

The equipment this operator had consisted of the following:

        2 - jacks
        1 - combination skiver and sole cutter
        1 - heel remover
        1 - splitter
        1 - Goodyear welt stitcher
        1 - 12 foot finisher
        1 - patching machine
        1 - 2 pair cement press
        1 - tempering box
            and an assortment of hand tools

In this set up the cementing machine was on casters and rolled under the work bench, under the heel remover.

Tempering box was located under the combination sole cutter and skiver.

(Figure 181)

Shop Floor Plan

1. Display window
2. Stitcher
3. Finisher
4. Patching machine
5. Shelving for shoes
6. Sole cutter and skiver
7. Heel remover
8. Jacks
9. Work bench
10. Cash register
11. Accessory shelves
12. Waiting booths
13. Accessory display
14. Shine chair

Scale 1/8 inch = 1 foot

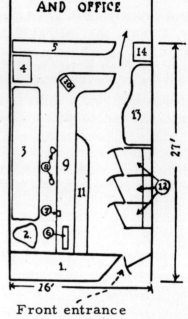

Front entrance

The stock of leather, taps and heels was under work bench by the jacks.

It will be noted that the finisher set directly be-hind the jacks. This was done because sanding wheels are used by jackmen throughout all jacking operations. Operators merely had to pivot from jack to sanding wheels.

Equipment and materials should be placed as near operator as possible, according to frequency of use.

LESSON   XXVII

SUGGESTIONS FOR SHOP OPERATIONS

Keep the walls and ceiling of your store painted in light colors, for example, creams, tans, pastel shades of other colors, etc.

Keep your store well lighted with modern fixtures at all times. To keep abreast of the times in color schemes for your place, copy color combinations used by popular ladies stores of different types. This is suggested as the majority of your customers will be women - so make your place attractive to them.

Have only modern fixtures. Just any old counter, shelving or chairs are not attractive. Have all the fixtures harmonize - build along the same pattern and finished alike. New and modern fixtures will cost a little more at first but they will pay for themselves in the long run.

Remember, the appearance of a business establishment is the making or breaking of the place.

Keep your machinery clean and fresh appearing at all times. Repaint it at least once a year.

Keep all your fixtures dusted at all times. There is nothing so provoking to a customer as soiling clothing in a business establishment. Keeping a place clean takes time but it pays dividends.

As mentioned before, keep your window trimmed regularly. It will cost you a little but people going by your place of business don't know what you're selling unless you show them. Most manufacturers of the products you sell and use, furnish window displays - get them and use them for they will work for you. Many manufacturers send display men around to trim your window for you - cooperate with him for you'll be surprised what he can do for you. If you can't trim the window yourself, there are available in practically every city display companies that can be retained to keep your window for you. Take advantage of your window for rent is based on the location and frontage of the building. A customer is 2/3 sold when he walks in the door of a business - your advertising has got to do that two-thirds selling job.

Keep the outside of the window washed daily.   There is nothing as unsightly as a dirty window. If money is spent trimming the window, let it be seen.

If the space can possibly be found, have at least one or two shine chairs.   They are a big business getter besides giving you added profit. An alert shine boy can and will sell laces and other accessories while he is shining the customer's shoes.   The shine boy can also be utilized for keeping the store clean.

Carry in stock all shoe and foot accessories you can possibly squeeze in and display properly.   They require very little space and each dollar profit they give you is that much more profit you won't have to "whittle" out by hand. Make your store the headquarters for everything pertaining to shoes.   Keep in stock polishes and dressings for all colors and types of shoes. Carry laces of all colors and sizes.   Have in stock insoles, shoe trees, heel pads, shoe mitts, polish kits, brushes and any other items that pertain to footwear.   The profits from your accessory sales can easily take care of the cost of your overhead. Your jobber can and will be glad to help keep you posted on styles and stock levels.   Make your shop the footwear headquarters.

When ordering stock buy only what your anticipated needs will be. Pay your wholesale bills promptly. Take the discounts on your wholesale bills for the discounts are your profit.

Keep books! Know what it costs you to operate! Know what items are making money for you, and which ones are not. If certain items are losing money, it may be your fault. Maybe you are not "plugging" them enough. If the item is dead for your locality, get rid of it. You don't know these things unless you keep an accurate account of your entire business.

To figure the selling price of your shoe repair services follow this standard formula: -

1. Cost of materials - 1/3 of selling price
2. Overhead (rent, wages, power, heat, etc.) - 1/3 of selling price
3. Profits - 1/3 of selling price.

In other words, if you put on a pair of taps for $1.00 your materials (taps, nails, thread and cement) should cost about 33 1/3 cents. On this basis there should be no reason why you shouldn't make yourself a very nice profit, providing, you expend effort to get customers into your store.

Not only must you keep your establishment neat and attractive at all times, but you and your help must be neat at all times too. Start with your own shoes - be a walking advertisement for your business. Your help's shoes must be kept up at all times. Keep yourself well groomed at all times. Smile and be cheerful to your customers - a smile costs you nothing but pays big dividends.

Be popular in your community - be seen where people are - be active in your community activities - let people know who you are and what you do. A shoe-repairman must be as active in community affairs as any other type of business man.

Even though you have the best mouse trap in the world, unless you let people know you have it and where you have it - you will just have it.

Be always on the alert to how and what other businesses are doing. They may give you an idea for yours.

Subscribe to trade journals and study them for they are the "melting pot" of trade hints and new ideas. Remember the old adage, "Listen to everyone, for even a fool says something sometimes."

Index